W9-AVA-221

PRAISE FOR *THE SOUTHERN VEGETARIAN*

"True Southern food will always adapt to its surroundings. It is not the stubborn lout that many think it is; rather, it's a nimble cheerleader of its region. It revels in vegetables and cherishes seasons. Burks and Lawrence are adding healthy substance to the definition of our Southern food. *The Southern Vegetarian* is a great addition to any culinary library."

—HUGH ACHESON, AUTHOR, *A NEW TURN IN THE SOUTH*

"What you have in your hands is a gift. It is a fresh, fun, slightly irreverent and joyful new look at Southern vegetarian dishes . . . a look that needed to be taken."

—JOHN CURRENCE, RECIPIENT OF THE JAMES BEARD FOUNDATION AWARD FOR BEST CHEF SOUTH; CHEF/OWNER, CITY GROCERY RESTAURANT GROUP

"Come eat with The Chubby Vegetarian. Justin and Amy are the only people I have ever met who can take the hock out of greens and not remove the soul from the pot."

—CHEF KELLY ENGLISH, *FOOD & WINE* BEST NEW CHEF 2009; CHEF/OWNER, THE AWARD-WINNING *RESTAURANT IRIS*

"Justin and Amy have a reverent respect for the traditions of Southern cooking and a bold adventurousness about its evolving future. In addition to cracking the code for a perfect cheese dip, they're sharing dozens of instant classics in these beautiful and smartly written pages."

—NICK ROGERS, FOOD WRITER AND FOUNDER OF THE WORLD CHEESE DIP CHAMPIONSHIP

"If Justin and Amy were my personal chefs, even a bacon lover like me could be a vegetarian. There is a joie de vivre to their cooking because they mix heart and home into a scrumptious cornucopia for everyone."

—PAMELA DENNEY, FOOD EDITOR, *MEMPHIS MAGAZINE*

"Justin and Amy are smart, fun, and creative, and that shines through in their recipes. No need to miss meat—each dish showcases an incredible fruit or vegetable with innovative flavor combinations, approachable techniques, and a touch of Southern flair."

—MELISSA PETERSEN, EDITOR, *EDIBLE MEMPHIS*

"Justin and Amy's new book has a permanent place on my kitchen counter. Their enthusiasm and love of all things veggie gave me the inspiration to go meatless several days a week."

—JENNIFER CHANDLER, AUTHOR, *SIMPLY GRILLING*

THE **SOUTHERN**
VEGETARIAN
COOKBOOK

THE SOUTHERN VEGETARIAN COOKBOOK

100 DOWN-HOME RECIPES FOR THE MODERN TABLE

JUSTIN FOX BURKS & AMY LAWRENCE

THOMAS NELSON
Since 1798

NASHVILLE   DALLAS   MEXICO CITY   RIO DE JANEIRO

Published in Nashville, Tennessee, by Thomas Nelson. Thomas Nelson is a registered trademark of Thomas Nelson, Inc.

Thomas Nelson, Inc., titles may be purchased in bulk for educational, business, fund-raising, or sales promotional use. For information, please e-mail SpecialMarkets@ThomasNelson.com.

Library of Congress Cataloging-in-Publication Data

Burks, Justin Fox.
  The Southern vegetarian cookbook : 100 down-home recipes for the modern table / Justin Fox Burks and Amy Lawrence.
    pages cm
  Includes bibliographical references and index.
  ISBN 978-1-4016-0482-0 (pbk.)
  1. Cooking, American—Southern style. 2. Vegetarian cooking. I. Lawrence, Amy. II. Title.
  TX715.2.S68B874 2013
  641.5'6360975—dc23   2012041487

Printed in the United States of America

14 15 16 17 18 QG 6 5 4 3

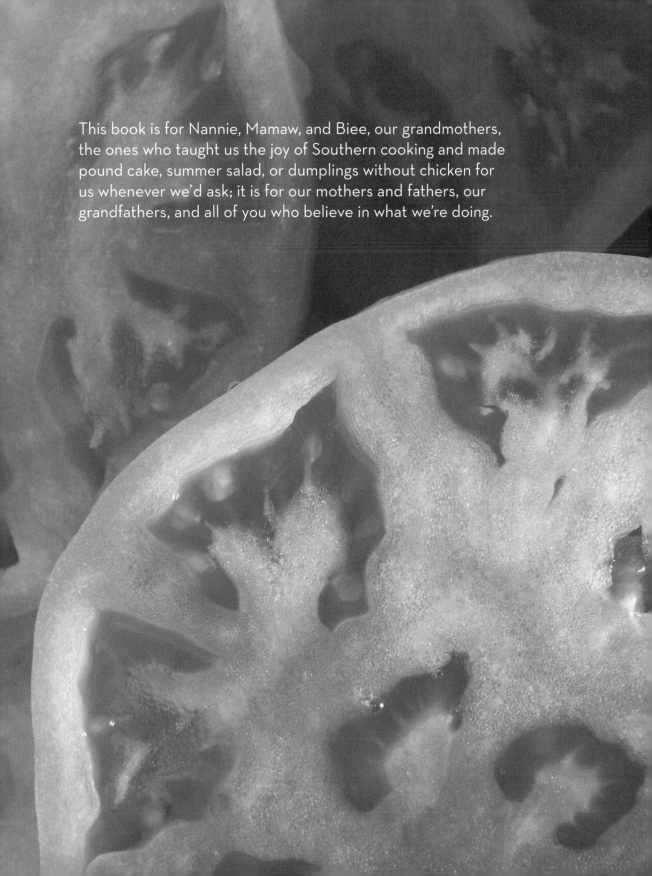

This book is for Nannie, Mamaw, and Biee, our grandmothers, the ones who taught us the joy of Southern cooking and made pound cake, summer salad, or dumplings without chicken for us whenever we'd ask; it is for our mothers and fathers, our grandfathers, and all of you who believe in what we're doing.

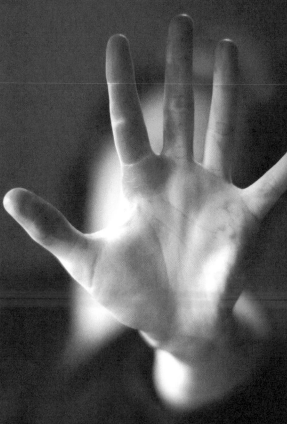

CONTENTS

A Forward Foreword by Chef John Currence **xi**

Introduction **xiii**

Essential Kitchen Tools **xv**

The Well-Stocked Vegetarian Pantry **xvii**

Breakfast and Brunch **1**

Appetizers and Salads **27**

Soups and Sandwiches **75**

Main Courses **117**

Desserts **177**

Drinks **205**

Basic Recipes **221**

Thank You So Much, Y'all **235**

About the Authors **237**

Index **238**

A FORWARD FOREWORD

by Chef John Currence

S o here's a little something few people know about me: for about six or eight months in 1986 during my tenure at UNC, I posed as a vegetarian. I say "posed" because, as much as I wanted to impress that very special young lady in my life, I knew all along I was a fraud . . . a terrible, hypocritical, meat-loving fraud.

I wore my façade nobly. I had just started cooking professionally, so I soldiered stoically through bacon-heavy shifts at Crook's Corner and absorbed occasional chiding. I girded myself for visits home to unrelenting attacks from my dad and brother, who both still have fun with my "phase" to this day, almost thirty years later.

How I returned to carnivore-ism is a subject of mystery. Whether it was my inability to withstand the draw of a corn dog at the North Carolina State Fair or a muffuletta given to me in my weakened condition by a friend, the reason is lost at this point, but what I do know is that my status was surrendered because I knew I just didn't belong among a noble few. I didn't care about the animal lives sacrificed. I was well aware that the diet was not necessarily any healthier than a meat-peppered one. And I was heartbroken, so I was returning to my old ways.

As a budding line cook, I was part of a vitriolic pirates' movement in the kitchens I worked in during the 1980s. Vegetarian requests were met with profanity-laced insults of the infidel who would make such demands. We begrudgingly assembled vegetable plates and sent them out with even less ceremony. Our places were temples of flesh, and those who came to worship our ability to manipulate muscle were adored. All others were nothing more than nuisance.

So, when I opened my first restaurant, City Grocery, in Oxford, Mississippi, in 1992, in my mind, the kitchen would be the rogue-est of any I had ever worked in. Testosterone bled from the walls, Gun and Roses blared from a stereo twice as big as the room needed, and NOBODY questioned our combinations or dish design. The wait staff were terrified to submit special orders, split plate requests, and, most of all, vegetarian queries. It was no way to run a kitchen, and I realized it very quickly.

The order of the day became, quickly, that special requests and vegetarian considerations be given the same respect as any other order to come into the kitchen. It was in these months, coincidentally, that my food was beginning to take shape. I was beginning to understand what my place was in the South and how that informed what I was trying to create, both with the food I was making and the place we were serving it.

A significant part of what my food spoke to was directly related to time I spent working with my maternal grandparents in their vegetable garden during the summers of my childhood. We harvested in the mornings, processed midday, canned in the afternoons, and stored in the evenings. It was a daily ritual, and though it was definitely not what inspired me to become a chef, it ultimately gave me the ability to understand and respect those things we worked so hard to grow and preserve.

It was a brush with death that finally brought me to full appreciation of the vegetable. I was sidelined with a case of pancreatitis in the summer of 2009. It is a catastrophically painful condition, and there is little that they can do for it other than starve you and pray. Mine was brought on by poor diet and even poorer genetics, it turns out. As it became clear what had happened to me, the immediate concern was whether I would ever consider food or cook it the same way again.

Though I had begun the process of lightening our food somewhat in the several years prior, I began in earnest as soon as I was able to get back to work. Vegetables took on a new significance, and again our food and attitude toward it changed.

It didn't hurt matters that in these dark porcine days, chefs across the country were loading everything they could think of with bacon to be more "Southern." For those of us growing up with and appreciating all parts of the pig and understanding how and where each piece of that animal was best used, it became an embarrassment that the long-awaited interest in Southern food was being immediately compartmentalized as little more than a pork-centric flash fascination.

The American South was, until the 1940s, the absolute breadbasket of vegetable production. There is nowhere in the country that can boast as rich a tradition of vegetable cultivation and perhaps family garden tending as the South. There are generations of family seed savers who swapped heirloom varieties and helped neighbors when there was crop failure or drought or whatever of the dozens of things that could go wrong did go wrong. Vegetables are our community.

This is what I love about food now. I revel in understanding and feeling why these things matter to us and how they guided us to where we are, and as a result, our kitchens don't look at vegetarians as adversaries now. Our non-meat-eating guests provide us with a unique opportunity at every order to celebrate that corner of the culinary landscape that is as Southern as anything else you may argue.

What you have in your hands is a gift. It is a fresh, fun, slightly irreverent and joyful new look at Southern vegetarian dishes . . . a look that needed to be taken. Justin and Amy aren't hemmed in by any of the tired clichés or stereotypical humorless dishes frequently found in "vegetarian" cookbooks. This tome is just playful while entirely on point in its objective. And what's more, the grand melting pot of the South is embraced as these recipes touch everything from traditional American to Latin to Indian to Asian and beyond, illustrating the magnificent tapestry that makes up the food of our corner of the country. It is simply exciting and vital.

So, now, run—do not walk—to your closest farmers' market, CSA, or local vegetable stand, arm yourself with whatever is in season, flip through these pages, and eat your vegetables. You'll be very happy that you did.

Radishes with softened butter are WAY underappreciated.

INTRODUCTION

To us, every meal feels like a celebration. Every time we cook, we celebrate our moms and dads and grandmothers and grandfathers, the people who taught us everything about preparing and then relishing a great meal together. We celebrate the friends and family crowded into our kitchen and gathered around our table, and we celebrate the wonderful textures and flavors available to us in the South. We celebrate creativity and passion, and finally, we celebrate our loved ones by preparing food that nourishes not only our bodies but also our souls.

The food in these pages speaks definitively about who we are and where we're from. We hope there is also a glimpse into where we are all headed in the future. Both of us are native Mississippians from outside of Jackson and the Delta town of Greenwood. We've lived in Memphis, Tennessee, since we were very young. We are Southerners to the core, but as you'll see, pretty far from the usual Southern stereotypes.

The South has always been a place focused on meats and sweets and known for its ribs, cookouts, and just plain old decadent cuisine. When we were growing up, it was almost certain some kind of meat would be hiding in all the vegetables on our plates. Today, every social event still revolves around who's bringing a dish and what will be served, but lately, there's been a subtle change in many Southerners' attitudes and actions. The connection has been made between the food we choose to eat, our overall health, and the health of our environment. There are vegetarian dishes at great soul food restaurants like De Javu in South Memphis and even an excellent vegetarian BBQ mushroom sandwich at the very popular Central BBQ.

The recipes in this book are close to our hearts. Most are updated versions of the food that has always been in our lives. There are unspoiled classics like Nannie's Blueberry Pie, Okra Fritters, and Summer Salad. There are also plenty of new twists on time-honored Southern dishes, such as our Fried Green Tomato Po' Boy, Mascarpone Banana Pudding, and BBQ Tofu Pizza. What we aim to do is move vegetables from the side of the plate straight to center stage. For example, instead of shrimp and grits, a dish you'll find all over the Carolina Low Country and in upscale restaurants in New Orleans, we give you Artichoke Hearts and Succotash over Smoked Cheddar Grits.

Don't worry. We don't aim to take your bacon away; we just want you to eat your vegetables. Our goal is to help you shape whole foods into hearty, tasty dishes that you'd be proud to serve your family and your friends at your own celebrations. This is vegetarian food that doesn't seem like vegetarian food. It's just good food that happens to be meatless.

We do love the old ways, but they needed some serious tweaking in order to make traditional Southern fare more healthful and decidedly more modern. We were determined to find a way to cook and eat Southern food that makes us feel great, and honestly, we had to figure it out as we went along.

We speak from experience when we tell you that simply cutting meat from your diet won't make you thin. In the space of a few years, we lost a combined one hundred pounds by refocusing our diet on vegetables, grains, and fruit—with the occasional over-the-top dinner (and usually, a dessert too!). It was trying at times—breaking old habits and forming new ones always is—but it wasn't as painful as we'd thought it would be. Hunger wasn't an issue. And really, no deprivation was involved. The connection between eating and exercising became clear, and from this emerged our new focus on satisfying from-scratch meals. But that isn't all we did.

We got active. Running, biking, yoga, swimming, and dance all found their way onto our weekly schedules and became mainstays. Most of all, we found balance: the balance between good eating and exercise that yielded the results we wanted. We also found an appreciation for each bite of food we put into our mouths.

Not one of our recipes starts with a stick of butter, and we try to limit the number of things we fry, which is an anomaly down South. But this isn't all health food; be assured, our version of the venerable Southern staple cheese dip won't save anyone. This collection of recipes is Southern food with its toes pointed in the right direction. Every dish is a part of who we are and where we come from. When you check out our recipes, we hope they inspire you. Surprise the family with a French Toast Pancake for Sunday brunch. Make some Red Beans and Rice with Andouille Eggplant for the ones you love. Try the Roast Beet Salad with Sea Salt Granola before supper. Celebrate the multitude of vegetables available at your farmers' market. Celebrate your health, and nourish those around you. Gather around your table, and celebrate it all along with us.

—Justin Burks Fox and Amy Lawrence

ESSENTIAL KITCHEN TOOLS

The most important element you need to cook a delicious meal is your desire to take care of yourself and the ones you love. That said, good, basic tools can make your time in the kitchen go more smoothly and quickly than you might imagine. Preparing to work in the kitchen is the most difficult part, but once you're ready, you really can cook anything. These are the tools we use every day:

A GOOD, SHARP CHEF'S KNIFE: We love our Global 8-inch chef's knife and Hammer Stahl santoku knife. A good knife will last a lifetime if it's taken care of properly, so never wash it in the dishwasher; only rinse it with soapy water and wipe it clean. In addition, store it in a knife block to keep it from getting dinged up in a drawer. We also have a few inexpensive ceramic knives in regular rotation.

A GOOD-QUALITY FOOD PROCESSOR: Save for a knife, this is our favorite kitchen tool. It saves so much time by doing a good deal of chopping, cutting, slicing, and mixing for us. We even make pizza dough and pie crust in it. We use the Cuisinart 14-cup food processor nearly every day and have spotted the same model in more than one professional kitchen.

A WELL-CONSTRUCTED, MOSTLY METAL BLENDER: The Hamilton Beach Commercial model has never let us down, and we have burned through many lesser blenders in the past. Look for a stainless steel cup and metal gears.

A SET OF STAINLESS STEEL MEASURING CUPS AND MEASURING SPOONS: Whether you're following a recipe or writing your own, a good set of measuring cups and spoons is key to the success of your dish. Dry ingredients should be spooned into the measuring cups and spoons and then leveled off with a knife.

A LIQUID MEASURING CUP: Liquid ingredients should be measured using a clear cup with measurements marked on the side. Follow this technique and you'll have accurate measurements every time.

AN 8-QUART STOCKPOT: Look for one that is heavy and preferably made out of stainless steel. Make sure it comes with a lid that fits tightly. It will last a lifetime if it's cared for properly. We received the All-Clad stockpot as a gift, and we love it.

A 10-INCH AND A 12-INCH FRYING PAN: All-Clad makes a set of these two particular sizes of pans, which can usually be found for under a hundred dollars. They will never warp or wear out, and there is no coating to chip off. Simply use a tablespoon of salt and a paper towel to clean any stubborn bits. You can even wash them in the dishwasher. We also like Bialetti Aeternum pans for scrambled eggs and omelets.

AN IMMERSION BLENDER: This tool is indispensable when we're making sauces and soups and want a silky-smooth texture. It also keeps us from having to transfer hot liquid into a blender, which can be a dangerous task. We have the Hamilton Beach Smart Stick, which is accompanied by a few useful attachments.

A 3-QUART SAUCEPAN WITH LID: Grits, rice, sauces, and a million other things will be made beautifully in this mid-sized saucepan. It's nice to have two of these on hand in case you're working on a dish with multiple components. Make sure you find one that's heavy for its size and comes with a lid. We own a few different models of this stainless steel pan, and they all perform well.

KITCHEN TONGS: Think of these as an extension of your hand. We use ours every day to turn items in the frying pan or flip items on the grill, and we even stir with them if they're handy. They're just good for everything and are really inexpensive. Get the plain aluminum tongs; they're available at any kitchen supply store.

PARCHMENT PAPER: This item is indispensable in our kitchen. Line baking sheets with it to make sure nothing sticks. Roll out pizza dough on it for a foolproof way to slide your pizza into the oven with no problems at all. For baking anything from cookies to bread, it's a game-changer in the kitchen. It saves on both oil usage and clean-up time.

A BENCH SCRAPER: We use this as a multi-tool. If we have a bunch of chopped vegetables that need to be transferred to a pot, we grab the bench scraper. We also use it for its intended purpose, to scrape dough off of a cutting board. For quick clean-up, it works well on butcher blocks and cutting boards.

A SET OF 17 X 12-INCH RIMMED BAKING SHEETS: Whether we're making a big batch of mushroom meat, baking our favorite biscuits, or browning cookies, these workhorse pans are all we need.

LARGE AND SMALL SPRING-ACTION ICE-CREAM SCOOPS: Believe it or not, we rarely use these to scoop ice cream. Rather, they're great for portioning veggie burger patties, ravioli filling, cookies, or muffins.

A SERRATED PEELER: It's really the only peeler we use. The serrated blade allows us to easily peel soft vegetables like tomatoes and peaches. It's also good for peeling just about everything else.

AN OUTDOOR GRILL: If you don't own an outdoor grill, frankly, you're doing yourself a disservice as a home cook. The open flame adds so much flavor to everything it touches. We use ours to smoke tomatoes, mushrooms, and peaches, as well as to grill up a mess of eggplant or make Smoky Grilled Vegetable Quesadillas.

A PIZZA STONE: We keep one in the oven at all times. It helps regulate the temperature, and there is no substitute for a hot pizza stone when you're making pizza or bread in a home oven.

A GRATER AND ZESTER: We have one for zesting citrus and one for grating hard cheeses, and honestly, we wouldn't want to cook without both of them within reach. They make these two kitchen tasks a breeze.

ADDITIONAL ITEMS: Other helpful items include a few stainless steel mixing bowls, silicone spatulas, whisks of all sizes, metal spatulas, a box grater, a colander, small prep bowls, glass food storage containers, wire cooling racks, and a couple of cutting boards.

There are some other special tools used in our recipes, where we will list any special equipment.

THE WELL-STOCKED VEGETARIAN PANTRY

A well-stocked pantry is essential for anyone who plans to spend quality time in the kitchen. Nothing is more frustrating than feeling like you need to run to the grocery store for an item every time you start to cook. What follows is a list of basic ingredients that are great to have on hand whether you're whipping up a meal or trying out a recipe for the first time.

FATS

In the South we have a saying, "The flavor comes from fat," but we also know that we have to be moderate with those fats in order to stay healthy. It's important to choose things like olive oil and canola oil, which are low in saturated fat. Olive oil is our go-to for most salad dressings and main courses; however, it isn't great for panfrying because of its low smoke point. Canola oil has a high smoke point, so it's perfect for crisping up vegetables in a hot pan or frying. It's also great in muffins and desserts due to its clean, light flavor.

Whenever we use butter, we use unsalted butter. Salted butter makes it difficult to gauge how much salt is going into the dish. Butter adds that undeniable, rich flavor to things like our Tofu Almondine in a White Wine-Butter Sauce and our Strawberry-Basil Shortcakes.

Soy or olive oil margarine are also a staple in our fridge. It's wonderful to use in baking and even tastes great on something as simple as a piece of French bread.

Spectrum brand organic non-hydrogenated vegetable shortening is our number one choice for making piecrusts, pound cake, and biscuits. Nothing else works quite like it.

Black truffle oil is nice to have in the kitchen. A drop or two can make a meal unique. Keep specialty fats like this one—and other good choices such as almond, walnut, and hazelnut oils—in the fridge, where they will keep longer.

FLOURS AND STARCHES

Flours and starches typically serve as the stage on which the other flavors shine, but their role is equally important. Nothing beats a homemade biscuit, handmade pasta, or a nice big bowl of grits. We keep all-purpose flour, bread flour, and whole wheat pastry flour lined up in the baking cabinet so we're ready for anything.

We use yellow corn grits to make traditional Southern grits. Cornmeal is a finer grind and is used to make cornbread, among other things.

Garbanzo bean flour may seem a bit exotic, but it's fairly easy to find these days. We use it to whip up little fritters for an easy lunch, and it's also great for thickening soups.

Don't waste your money buying regular old bread crumbs. We have no problem keeping our pantry stocked with this staple by using old bread that we first toast in the oven until it's dry and then turn into crumbs using the food processor.

RICE AND PASTA

It's nice to keep at least one kind of rice and one kind of pasta in the pantry. We usually keep brown rice for those times when we're feeling virtuous—and when we have 40 minutes to cook it. Jasmine rice is also a key item for us because it's quick-cooking, as well as fragrant and delicious. Specialty rice like Carolina Gold is good to use when a regional recipe calls for something more specific.

Whenever we're unsure about what to make for dinner, the answer is always some variation of pasta. So we keep plenty of thin spaghetti noodles, rigatoni, orzo, and fettuccini around for a quick and stress-free meal.

NUTS

Unsalted nuts are such a great source of protein for vegetarians. They also add so much texture to everything from salads to chili. We keep lots of almonds (sliced and whole), pecans, walnuts, and dry roasted peanuts around. Peanut butter, chocolate hazelnut butter, and almond butter are key ingredients as well. Nuts make a great snack too. We go through plenty of them each week, so we keep them in our pantry in mason jars, but if you have a large stock that will take you longer than a few months to eat, it's best to keep them in the fridge so the oil in the nut doesn't turn rancid.

BEANS

We try not to use many cans of food, so most days, it's dried beans all the way for us. Beans are so important in our diet because the combination of beans and rice creates a complete protein with all of the essential amino acids that our bodies need. We always have a selection of beans on hand. We love black beans, pinto beans, and that very Southern staple, black-eyed peas. Lentils, especially the brown and red varieties, are great because they cook so quickly. We often substitute lentils for other beans because they're so tasty and easy to cook. Make an extra-large batch of beans and store the leftover beans in a food storage container in the refrigerator or just freeze them if you need to keep them longer than a week.

SWEETENERS

For everyday use in coffee and most baked goods, we use vegan cane sugar, which skips the whitening process and never comes into contact with animal bones. We use brown rice syrup for making granola and agave nectar in our sweet tea. Light brown sugar usually finds its way into our BBQ sauce, while powdered sugar is great for frosting. A squeeze of local honey adds balance to any salad dressing, and maple syrup plays a key role in our Smoked Coconut Bacon.

SAUCES AND CONDIMENTS

Refrigerated sauces and pastes are a great way to add instant depth to any dish. We keep an arsenal of hot sauces to use in cooking or as a condiment. Chunky sambal and smooth sriracha are our favorite hot sauces for cooking because they add not only heat but flavor as well. In years past, they were hard to find, but now these two sauces can be found in almost any grocery store. We also love Tabasco for Louisiana spice and Valentina Black hot sauce for a Mexican kick.

Humble tomato paste can make all the difference in the world when added to chili or tomato sauce. Use it in conjunction with fresh tomatoes for a one-two punch.

Having a bottle of Zatarain's Creole Mustard is almost like cheating. Anything it touches turns to gold. We wouldn't trade it for anything.

We've been using Bragg Liquid Aminos for years now. We can't really tell the difference between it and soy sauce, but Bragg's has added amino acids that count as good nutrition.

Spectrum Olive Oil Mayonnaise makes a great base for our pimento cheese and is outstanding in our Caesar dressing. A little of this good stuff goes a long way.

Traditionally, Worcestershire sauce has anchovies in it, so look for bottles labeled "vegetarian Worcestershire sauce." A few drops in soups and stews can give the dish that savory underpinning that the tastebuds love.

We just recently made friends with liquid smoke, which is actually a natural product made of water, smoke, vinegar, and molasses. When smoking something on your outdoor grill isn't an option, this is the next-best thing. Smoke may be one of the most important flavors in Southern cooking, so this stuff is great to have on hand.

MILK AND CREAM

Depending on the recipe, we use organic 2% milk, half and half, or heavy cream.

VINEGAR

Vinegar may be the most underutilized ingredient in the home kitchen. Restaurant chefs know that the brightness brought forth by the acid in vinegar can enliven a dish and wake up your taste buds. We have lots of vinegars to choose from in our cabinet—everything from regular white vinegar to mild rice vinegar. A favorite is champagne vinegar because of its fruity nose, but balsamic vinegar and apple cider vinegar have their proper uses as well.

SPICES

Most people get one of those spice racks with a million spices that they may never touch. We recommend buying little jars and filling them with the spices you know you'll use. For us, it's thyme, dill, paprika, smoked paprika, Italian seasoning, coriander seed, ground coriander, cumin, rubbed sage, garlic powder, red pepper flakes, ancho chili powder, clove, nutmeg, cinnamon, ginger, cayenne, chipotle, allspice, curry, Old Bay, and cream of tartar.

Vanilla beans are a splurge, but we keep a few on hand as there's no other way to get the true essence of vanilla into baked or steeped items. We also make our own vanilla extract by splitting the beans and allowing them to soak in vodka for a couple of months. Vanilla paste and vanilla powder are not always easy to find, but they are great for baking and in ice cream because of their concentrated flavor and visual appeal.

RAPID-RISE YEAST

Frankly, we just don't have the patience that's required when using any other type of yeast.

SALT AND PEPPER

We consistently have two kinds of salt in our kitchen: Maldon sea salt flakes and iodized salt. We use Maldon for just about everything except salting pasta water and dough or cleaning frying pans. The unabrasive, ocean-y flavor it provides is just right. A dish is best when it is slightly under-salted when being prepared and then lightly sprinkled with Maldon at the very end. The salt retains a nice crunch and provides little bursts of flavor. Morton coarse Kosher salt is also a stellar option. We also love hickory smoked sea salt and black truffle salt to add a burst of unexpected flavor. Use specialty flavored salts to finish a dish so that the flavor is more pronounced.

Pepper is a little bit simpler. First, forget all the pink-and-green, brown-and-black mixed peppercorns. It looks pretty, but that's too many competing flavors! Having Tellicherry black peppercorns in the grinder does make a difference on top of a finished dish. This pepper is big, strong, floral, and pungent.

STOCK

Making your own stock is great, but who has time every week to do this? Box stock or broth is the biggest single time-saver in the kitchen. We also like to keep a few vegetarian bouillon cubes on hand. They are perfect when you want to add flavor to a stock or broth but skip the liquid.

COOKING WINE

We always keep a box of Pinot Grigio white wine in the fridge. Nothing is better for deglazing a pan while adding a bit of acidity and sweetness, and it really helps to bring any dish to life.

PRODUCE

In the refrigerator, we like to keep the following items: peeled garlic, celery, carrots, peeled shallots, flat-leaf parsley, and fresh thyme. Stored properly, all of these items will keep for weeks.

Outside the refrigerator in a dark cabinet, we store sweet potatoes, Yukon Gold potatoes, and sweet onions; they'll keep for months. These are great items to stock up on at the farmers' market so that you have them on hand when you need them.

Regular lemons and Meyer lemons are must-have items, and limes and oranges will come in handy as well. If you're using citrus zest, ideally it should be from organic fruit.

In the fruit bowl, we always have Pink Lady and Granny Smith apples, tomatoes, avocados, and bananas.

BREAKFAST AND BRUNCH

Sweet Potato Grits with Maple Mushrooms and a Fried Egg   3

Southern Benedict with Wilted Spinach and Espresso Redeye Gravy   5

Miracle Mushroom Gravy   8

Smoked Sun-Dried Tomato Tortilla with Herbed Aioli   10

Simple Smoky Migas Bowl   12

Apple, Cheddar, and Thyme Galette   14

Sweet Potato Pancakes with Peaches and Pecans   17

French Toast Pancake   18

Super-Moist Banana Muffins   20

Toasted Coconut Muffins   22

Vegan Bran Muffins   24

SWEET POTATO GRITS WITH MAPLE MUSHROOMS AND A FRIED EGG

It's certainly arguable that all true Southerners adore grits; our version adds sweet potatoes for more creaminess and sweetness but still walks a fine line between sweet and savory. Feel free to serve this dish for breakfast, brunch, lunch, or dinner because it'll be a definite crowd favorite anytime.

Sweet Potato Grits (recipe follows)	Maple Mushrooms (recipe follows)	Sea salt flakes and cracked black pepper (to taste)
Parsley and Tomato Topping (recipe follows)	1 tablespoon unsalted butter 4 large eggs	

Make the grits, topping, and mushrooms according to the following recipes. Once you have the three recipes completed, follow these simple instructions to assemble your meal: Melt the butter in a 12-inch frying pan over medium heat. Crack eggs into the pan one at a time. Cover and cook for 5 minutes or until the white has set and the yolk is still runny. Divide the grits between four bowls. Top each with a fried egg, a sprinkling of the Parsley and Tomato Topping, and finally, the Maple Mushrooms. Add salt and pepper to finish.

Makes 4 servings.

SWEET POTATO GRITS

1 medium sweet potato	Sea salt flakes (to taste)	1 tablespoon unsalted butter
2 cups 2% milk	¼ teaspoon cracked black pepper	¼ to ½ cups vegetable stock or water
½ cup yellow corn grits		

Bake the sweet potato in a 350 degree F. oven for one hour. Remove and allow to cool. Once the potato is cool, the skin should peel right off. Slowly bring the milk up to a boil in a medium sauce-pan. Whisk in the grits a little at a time to avoid clumps. Add 1 cup of the baked sweet potato and break it up with your whisk. (Be careful—hot grits tend to bubble like lava. Use an oven mitt when stirring your grits just to be safe.) Add the salt, pepper, and butter; lower the heat to medium-low.

Grits take 10 to 20 minutes to cook and become silky and supple. This all depends on the corn and how coarse the grind is. Taste them after 10 minutes to make sure they're soft and creamy since the ideal cooking time for different brands of grits varies. Stir occasionally. Use stock or water to achieve the desired consistency. Don't worry—grits are rarely overcooked.

Makes 4 cups.

PARSLEY AND TOMATO TOPPING

1 cup diced tomato (about 1 medium)

¼ teaspoon cane sugar

Sea salt flakes and cracked black pepper (to taste)

¼ cup chopped parsley

¼ cup minced shallots

Mix the tomato, sugar, salt, pepper, parsley, and shallots together in a bowl. Set aside until ready to use.

Makes 1 ½ cups.

MAPLE MUSHROOMS

¼ cup maple syrup

¼ cup canola oil

1 teaspoon cracked black pepper

1 ½ teaspoons grainy mustard

2 tablespoons soy sauce

½ teaspoon liquid smoke

1 (10-ounce) package crimini (baby bella) mushrooms, sliced

In a medium bowl whisk together the maple syrup, canola oil, black pepper, mustard, soy sauce, and liquid smoke. Toss in the sliced mushrooms and allow to marinate for 20 minutes.

Preheat your oven to 350 degrees F. Drain the marinade and arrange the mushrooms in a single layer on a parchment-lined baking sheet. Cook for 20 minutes or until the mushrooms begin to brown and appear dry. Remove from the oven and allow to cool.

Maple mushrooms are great on this dish but can also be used on salads or in a vegetarian BLT. The same seasoning can be added to strips of portobello or shiitake mushrooms. Since these can be made ahead of time, it's a great idea to keep a batch around in order to add flavor to almost any dish. They will keep in an airtight container in the refrigerator for up to 3 days.

Makes 1 ½ cups.

SOUTHERN BENEDICT WITH WILTED SPINACH AND ESPRESSO REDEYE GRAVY

This looks like a lot to do first thing in the morning, but the steps are really simple. Plus, you'll make more biscuits than you'll need for this dish. You know what that means... snack while you cook!

The espresso in the gravy adds instant oomph. That paired with the mushrooms provides a super-savory gravy that you'll make again and again. Underneath, you have a poached egg with a runny yolk, plenty of wilted greens, and a craggy biscuit supporting the whole dish.

1 tablespoon iodized salt	4 3-2-1 Buttermilk Drop Biscuits (page 222)	Espresso Red-Eye Gravy (recipe follows)
¼ cup white vinegar	Wilted Spinach (recipe follows)	½ teaspoon smoked paprika (to garnish)
8 large eggs		

In a large pan over medium heat, bring an inch and a half of water to a simmer. Add the salt and vinegar to the water and return it to a simmer. Poach eggs three to four at a time by slowly cracking each egg into the simmering water and allowing it to cook for 5 minutes or until the white is set. Using a slotted spoon, remove each egg from the water and set it aside on a paper towel until ready to serve.

Split a buttermilk biscuit in half and place it open-faced onto a plate. Place ¼ cup of wilted spinach on each half. Top each half with a poached egg and about ¼ cup of the Red-Eye Gravy. Garnish with smoked paprika. Repeat.

Makes 4 servings.

WILTED SPINACH

1 tablespoon unsalted butter	12 ounces (two 6-ounce bags) fresh spinach	Sea salt flakes and cracked black pepper (to taste)
½ cup diced shallots		

Melt the butter in a medium pan over medium heat. Add the diced shallots and cook until translucent, about 3 minutes. Add the fresh spinach one handful at a time; stir the greens in between each addition so that the heat from the pan wilts them. Once the greens are wilted, turn off the heat, add salt and pepper, and set the pan aside.

Makes about 2 cups.

ESPRESSO REDEYE GRAVY

2 tablespoons unsalted butter (divided)

1 cup diced portobello mushrooms

¼ teaspoon cracked black pepper

¼ teaspoon red pepper flakes

Sea salt flakes (to taste)

¼ cup espresso (or strong coffee)

1 tablespoon all-purpose flour

1 ½ cups whole milk

⅛ teaspoon liquid smoke

1 teaspoon maple syrup

In a medium pan over medium-high heat, melt 1 tablespoon of butter. Add the mushrooms, black pepper, red pepper flakes, and salt to the pan, and cook until the mushrooms begin to brown, about 5 minutes. Add the espresso to deglaze the pan. Cook until most of the liquid has evaporated. Push the mushroom mixture off to one side of the pan. In the clearing add the remaining tablespoon of butter. Once it's melted, add the flour and whisk it into the butter. Allow this mixture to cook for a minute until the flour becomes fragrant. Whisk in the milk, liquid smoke, and maple syrup. Stir constantly until the mixture begins to boil. Reduce the heat to low and cook an additional 5 minutes until the mixture has thickened.

Makes about 2 cups.

MIRACLE MUSHROOM GRAVY

This wonderful vegetarian gravy has all the bold, spicy flavor of the sausage-based kind. We use meaty crimini mushrooms and the seasoning you'd normally find in a flavorful breakfast sausage to make our version of this Southern breakfast staple.

Try this on our Buttermilk 3-2-1 Drop Biscuits (page 222) for breakfast or on top of our Stuffed Acorn Squash (page 136).

1 (10-ounce) package crimini (baby bella) mushrooms

1 tablespoon canola oil

½ cup diced shallots

1 teaspoon dried sage

¼ teaspoon red pepper flakes

Scant ⅛ teaspoon ground clove

1 tablespoon soy sauce

1 tablespoon maple syrup

1 tablespoon unsalted butter

1 tablespoon all-purpose flour

1 ½ cups whole milk

Smoked paprika (to garnish)

Slice mushrooms about ¼ inch thick. You will blend them later, so there's no need to be overly precise. Add the canola oil to a medium frying pan over high heat and then sauté the mushrooms until browned. Add the shallots to the pan, and continue to cook for another minute until the rawness has been cooked out of the shallots and they're translucent.

Place the mushrooms and shallots into the work bowl of your food processor, and add the sage, red pepper flakes, clove powder, soy sauce, and maple syrup. In the same pan over medium heat, melt the butter and add the flour. Whisk the mixture until fragrant, about 5 minutes. Whisk in the whole milk and heat the mixture until slightly thick. Add the milk mixture to the food processor that contains the mushroom mixture. Pulse until the mushrooms are finely chopped and well incorporated into the milk, but leave some chunkiness for a nice texture. Return the mixture to the pan and keep warm until ready to serve. If it gets too thick, add some milk or stock to thin it out.

If having this gravy with biscuits, split the biscuits and top them with the mushroom gravy. Garnish each with a pinch of smoked paprika.

Makes 4 servings.

SMOKED SUN-DRIED TOMATO TORTILLA WITH HERBED AIOLI

When a person even mentions a recipe or dish, we lock in on it and have to try it too. Within seconds of meeting someone, the conversation almost always turns to food. We love to ask questions and gain inspiration from passionate, everyday cooking.

This is what gave me the idea to make a Spanish tortilla. At a photo shoot recently, I started asking people what they were making for dinner. One person told me that she was making a tortilla. I'd had some delicious versions of this potato-and-egg dish in the past. So as I drove home, all I could think about was what I would put in my own version of a Spanish tortilla. Here, smoked sun-dried tomatoes are the star.

Smoked sun-dried tomatoes can be found at many specialty grocery stores, or you could make a big batch using our Quick Smoking Method (page 231).

2 tablespoons olive oil

1 medium russet potato (peeled and sliced into ⅛-inch rounds)

6 large eggs

½ cup diced smoked sun-dried tomatoes

¼ cup 2% milk

½ cup minced shallots

Sea salt flakes and cracked black pepper (to taste)

2 ounces Manchego cheese, shredded, plus more for garnish

½ cup sliced garlic chives or green onions (to garnish)

2 to 3 tablespoons sriracha (to garnish)

Herbed Aioli (recipe follows)

Preheat your oven to 350 degrees F. Heat a 10-inch frying pan over high heat until it starts to smoke just a little. Add 2 tablespoons of olive oil and then add the potatoes in a single layer on the bottom of the skillet. Turn off the heat on the skillet, cover, and set aside for 5 minutes. The heat from the skillet will sear the outside of the potato, and the residual heat will cook them through.

Mix the eggs, sun-dried tomatos, milk, and minced shallot, and then pour this mixture over the potatoes. Top with salt, pepper, and cheese. Cover and place the skillet in the oven for 15 to 20 minutes or until the center is set. After running a knife around the edge of the tortilla, turn the tortilla over onto a serving plate so that the potato side faces up. Serve tortilla hot or at room temperature. Garnish each slice with a bit more cheese, garlic chives, sriracha, and Herbed Aioli.

Makes 4 servings.

HERBED AIOLI

1 ½ cups loose-packed parsley

1 medium clove garlic

Zest of 1 lemon

½ cup olive oil mayonnaise

Sea salt flakes and cracked black pepper (to taste)

Blend parsley, garlic, lemon zest, and olive oil mayonnaise until smooth. Add salt and pepper to taste. You may have some aioli left over to use on sandwiches or wraps. Store in the refrigerator for up to 5 days.

Makes about ¾ cups.

SIMPLE SMOKY MIGAS BOWL

1 tablespoon unsalted butter

4 large eggs (beaten)

½ cup Simple Smoky Salsa (page 223)

1 ½ cups corn chips

1 cup prepared white or brown rice

Seasoned Black Beans (recipe follows)

3 to 4 ounces soft goat cheese, crumbled

Cilantro leaves (to garnish)

4 small flour tortillas

Sea salt flakes and cracked black pepper to garnish

Melt butter in a medium pan over medium-low heat. Add the eggs and stir constantly using rubber spatula. Once the eggs come together, add the salsa and continue to scramble. Add the corn chips and mix to incorporate. Divide the rice among two serving bowls and top each with about ½ cup of the Seasoned Black Beans and then add half of the scrambled egg mixture to each bowl. Top with goat cheese and cilantro leaves. Serve with warm flour tortillas.

Makes 2 servings.

SEASONED BLACK BEANS

1 teaspoon canola oil

¼ cup diced shallot

¼ teaspoon granulated garlic

½ teaspoon sage

½ teaspoon cumin

1 (15-ounce) can black beans (drained, rinsed)

1 tablespoon white vinegar

½ cup broth or water

Sea salt flakes and cracked black pepper (to taste)

In a small saucepan over medium heat, add the canola oil, shallot, granulated garlic, sage, and cumin. Cook until fragrant. Add the beans, vinegar, and broth. Allow the beans to simmer for 5 minutes. Mash lightly with a potato masher. Add salt and pepper to taste. Cover and keep warm on the stove until ready to serve.

Makes about 1 ½ cups beans.

APPLE, CHEDDAR, AND THYME GALETTE

This is a more grown-up but still sneaky little way to have apple pie for breakfast. It's lightly sweet with only two tablespoons of brown sugar in the whole dish, and the cheese is baked right into the filling. The onion and thyme add to its savory qualities.

Juice of 1 lemon (about 2 teaspoons)

4 cups sliced apples (about 4 medium, peeled and sliced into ¼-inch slices)

1 tablespoon unsalted butter

2 cups sliced onion (about 1 medium)

¼ cup white wine (like Pinot Grigio)

1 ½ cups shredded sharp Cheddar cheese

1 tablespoon fresh thyme leaves (about 4 sprigs)

2 tablespoons firmly packed light brown sugar

Sea salt flakes and cracked black pepper (to taste)

Basic Piecrust Dough (page 227)

Preheat your oven to 375 degrees F. Place the lemon juice and apples in a large bowl. In a 10-inch skillet over medium-high heat, melt the butter and sauté the onion until translucent and beginning to brown, which should take 8 minutes. Add the wine and turn up the heat to medium-high in order to reduce the wine. Once most of the liquid has evaporated, remove the onion mixture from the pan and add it to the bowl with the apples. Toss together the Cheddar, thyme, brown sugar, salt, and pepper.

To assemble the galette, roll out the chilled dough on a lightly floured board to approximately a 17 x 12-inch oval. This is supposed to look rustic, so no need to be too precise. Place the dough on a 17 x 12-inch rimmed baking sheet lined with parchment paper. Pour the apple-Cheddar mixture into the center of the dough, and press it with your palms until it's evenly distributed, making sure to leave a 1 ½-inch margin around the edge. Fold the margin of the dough over in 2-inch sections overlapping the end of each section. This will hold in any juices.

Bake for 35 minutes or until the crust is golden brown and the apples on the top are caramelized.

Makes 4 servings.

SWEET POTATO PANCAKES WITH PEACHES AND PECANS

At the downtown farmers' market on Saturday morning, a coworker was so excited about going to the Arcade Restaurant in order to have their sweet potato pancakes for breakfast, and we just had to have some, too—from our own kitchen. These pancakes offer a silkiness that's different from the usual buttermilks or buckwheats.

1 cup roughly chopped sweet
   potato (about 1 large)

2 large eggs, beaten

1 ½ cups 2% milk

¼ cup soy or olive
   oil margarine or
   butter, softened

1 cup all-purpose flour

½ cup whole wheat
   pastry flour

3 tablespoons cane sugar

3 ½ teaspoons baking powder

½ teaspoon iodized sea salt

⅛ teaspoon of nutmeg

Toppings:

2 cups diced peaches
   (about 4 peaches)

1 teaspoon lemon juice

1 tablespoon cane sugar

1 cup pecans, toasted*
   and chopped

Unsalted butter

Maple syrup

Boil the sweet potato on medium-high for about 15 minutes in a saucepan with enough water to just cover it. Carefully test with a fork; when it's soft, it's ready. Pour the potato into a colander and run cold water over it. Using a potato masher or a fork, mash the potato well in a large bowl. Add the eggs, milk, and margarine.

In a medium bowl, whisk the all-purpose flour, whole wheat pastry flour, sugar, baking powder, salt, and nutmeg together. Add the flour mixture to the sweet potato and mix until just combined. Heat a griddle pan on medium-low, butter the pan, and pour ¼ cup of the batter onto the pan. Allow the pancake to cook until the top looks like it has set (about 3 minutes). Flip the pancake and allow it to cook for another minute. Repeat until all the batter has been used.

Next, combine the peaches, lemon juice, and sugar. Allow the peaches to macerate for at least 5 minutes.

To serve, pile a few pancakes on a plate, top with the peach mixture, and add chopped pecans, butter, and a drizzle of maple syrup.

Makes 4 servings (16 pancakes).

*Toast pecans by spreading them in a single layer on a plate and microwaving them for 30 seconds at a time (repeat three times) until they're fragrant.

FRENCH TOAST PANCAKE

Whenever we have an easygoing morning, one of us clamors for either pancakes or French toast. One morning, with little time to waste, we invented the super-fast French toast pancake. There's no agonizing wait for the egg-and-milk mixture to soak into the bread, it's very hands-off since it cooks in the oven, and the whole thing is done in two quick steps.

2 cups torn French bread

6 large eggs

Zest of 1 orange

1 teaspoon vanilla extract

½ cup whole milk

⅛ teaspoon iodized sea salt

1 tablespoon cane sugar

1 ½ tablespoons
  unsalted butter

Macerated fruit, butter,
  powdered sugar, and
  maple syrup (to garnish)

Preheat your oven to 350 degrees F. Place the bread, eggs, orange zest, vanilla, milk, salt, and sugar in the bowl of a food processor and pulse until there are no big chunks of bread left.

Heat a 12-inch oven-safe frying pan over medium-high heat. Place the butter into the hot pan and allow it to melt completely and coat the pan. Pour the egg and bread mixture into the pan. The hot pan will help the pancake start cooking and will prevent it from sticking.

Place the pan into the oven for 10 minutes or until the center is set. To serve, cut the pancake into wedges and top with your choice of macerated fruit, butter, powdered sugar, and maple syrup.

Makes 4 servings.

SUPER-MOIST BANANA MUFFINS

We wanted a banana muffin recipe that was really far away from dry and also fairly quick to put together. The center of these muffins resembles bread pudding partly because of the higher ratio of banana used.

3 ripe bananas, mashed
   (about 1 ½ cups)

3 tablespoons sour cream

1 egg, beaten

¼ cup unsalted
   butter, melted

¼ cup cane sugar

¼ cup light brown sugar

1 tablespoon honey

2 teaspoons vanilla extract

⅔ cup all-purpose flour

⅓ cup whole wheat flour

1 teaspoon iodized sea salt

1 teaspoon baking powder

Preheat your oven to 350 degrees F. Mix the bananas, sour cream, egg, butter, cane sugar, light brown sugar, honey, and vanilla. In another bowl whisk together the all-purpose flour, whole wheat flour, salt, and baking powder. Carefully fold the banana mixture into the flour mixture so the batter is just mixed. Pour the batter into a muffin tin lined with unbleached baking cups.

Bake the muffins for 35 minutes until the tops are crisp and lightly browned. Be sure to let them cool for at least 15 minutes.

Makes 12 muffins.

TOASTED COCONUT MUFFINS

It's easy to think ill of dried coconut. For some reason, we had a bag of unsweetened coconut flakes sitting in the cupboard for a while, and much to our surprise, it turned out to be an ingredient we actually ended up using a lot. Eat these muffins for breakfast as you imagine your perfect island vacation.

⅔ cup unsweetened
    coconut flakes

¾ cup whole wheat flour

¾ cup all-purpose flour

1 teaspoon baking powder

½ teaspoon sea salt flakes

¼ cup cane sugar

¼ cup firmly packed
    light brown sugar

⅓ cup brown rice syrup

1 large egg, beaten

2 ripe bananas, mashed
    (about a cup)

⅓ cup light coconut milk

⅓ cup sour cream

2 tablespoons soy or olive
    oil margarine, melted

2 tablespoons coconut oil

2 tablespoons dark rum

2 teaspoons vanilla extract

1 tablespoon canola oil

Salty, Sweet, and Crunchy
    Topping (recipe follows)

Preheat your oven to 350 degrees F. Toast the coconut flakes for about 10 minutes and set them aside to cool. In a large bowl, whisk together the whole wheat flour, all-purpose flour, baking powder, and sea salt. In a medium bowl stir together the cane sugar, light brown sugar, brown rice syrup, egg, and mashed bananas. To this, add the coconut milk, sour cream, margarine, coconut oil, dark rum, and vanilla.

Roughly chop the ⅔ cup toasted, cooled coconut. Gently fold together the flour mixture and banana mixture, along with the chopped coconut, but be careful not to overmix. Brush the muffin pan with canola oil and fill the cups almost to the top. Add the Salty, Sweet, and Crunchy Topping to the top of each muffin. Bake for 30 minutes or until a knife inserted into a tester muffin comes out clean with few crumbs.

Makes 12 muffins.

SALTY, SWEET, AND CRUNCHY TOPPING

3 tablespoons firmly packed
    light brown sugar

¼ cup unsweetened
    coconut flakes, chopped
    (not toasted)

¼ cup unsalted pecans,
    chopped

⅛ teaspoon sea salt flakes

1 tablespoon soy or
    olive oil margarine

Mix the light brown sugar, coconut flakes, pecans, and salt together in a small bowl. Sprinkle the mixture over each unbaked muffin, along with a dime-size sliver of margarine.

Makes about ¾ cup.

VEGAN BRAN MUFFINS

Oh, the lowly bran muffin: it can be like eating a scrap of kraft paper, or it can make being semi-virtuous really easy and palatable. Adding more bran and using whole wheat pastry flour and molasses give these muffins a deep, dark depth of flavor. If you want, mix up the batter ahead of time and store it covered in the fridge overnight; set out your muffin tin, liners, and an ice cream scoop before you go to bed, and you can have these warm from the oven on a weekday with very little morning-time effort at all.

1 ½ cups plain soy milk

1 ½ cups bran cereal

2 teaspoons vanilla extract

½ cup canola oil

2 tablespoons molasses
  or maple syrup

1 cup all-purpose flour

1 cup whole wheat
  pastry flour

1 teaspoon sea salt flakes

½ cup firmly packed
  light brown sugar

⅔ cup cane sugar

2 teaspoons baking soda

⅔ cup golden raisins

Salty and Sweet Topping
  (recipe follows)

Preheat your oven to 375 degrees F. In a medium bowl combine the soy milk and bran; let mixture sit for at least 10 minutes. Add the vanilla, canola oil, and molasses and stir. In a separate bowl, sift the all-purpose flour, whole wheat pastry flour, salt, light brown sugar, cane sugar, and baking soda. Combine the soy milk mixture and flour mixture; add raisins. Stir until just mixed. Use an ice-cream scoop to portion the batter into the muffin cups; they can be filled almost to level because they won't rise much. Add the Salty and Sweet Topping to the top of each muffin. Bake for 30 minutes or until a knife inserted into a tester muffin comes out clean with few crumbs.

Makes 12 muffins.

SALTY AND SWEET TOPPING

½ teaspoon sea salt flakes

1 tablespoon light
  brown sugar

1 tablespoon soy or
  olive oil margarine

Mix the salt and brown sugar in a small bowl. Sprinkle the mixture over each unbaked muffin, along with a dime-size sliver of margarine.

Makes about 2 tablespoons.

APPETIZERS AND SALADS

The Lime Truck's Corn Cake with BBQ Slaw   28

Natchitoches Umami Pies with Yogurt Chimichurri   31

Sambal Pepper Jelly and Savory Cheddar-Pecan Cookies   33

BBQ Tofu Nachos with Chipotle Pinto Beans and Guacamole   37

Green Pea Hummus   39

Okra Fritters with Creole Mustard Sauce   41

Oyster Mushroom Rockefeller   43

Mini Potato and Buttermilk Pancakes with Beluga Lentils and Crème Fraîche   46

Tofu and Truffle "Pork" Rinds   49

Zucchini Fries   50

Smoked Dates Stuffed with Goat Cheese and Pecans   53

Southern-Style Cheese Dip   54

Hoppin' John Black-Eyed Pea Butter   56

Deviled Egg and Olive   58

Grilled Watermelon and Tomato Salad with Honey-Lime Vinaigrette   61

Southern Caesar Salad with Cornbread Croutons   62

Summer Salad   65

Roast Beet Salad with Sea Salt Granola and Honey-Tarragon Dressing   67

Warm Brussels Sprout Salad with Smoked Feta and Candied Pecans   68

Caprese Salad in a Jar   70

Collard Greens (or Any Greens!) with Honey, Shallots, and Mushrooms   72

THE LIME TRUCK'S CORN CAKE WITH BBQ SLAW

We're so excited to present a recipe from Jason Quinn, formerly of the Lime Truck, from all the way out in California. As you may know, the Lime Truck won the second season of the Food Network's competition The Great Food Truck Race. *This dish was one they served as part of the vegetarian challenge I judged here in Memphis, and Jason was kind enough to share the recipe with me.*

The concept is simple but creative, and the execution is spot-on. Jason makes everything from scratch at his restaurant, the Playground, but he allowed me to use a couple of shortcuts here for the home cook. I could totally see making miniature versions of this dish for a party and serving them like little Southern blini. This recipe could serve 4 as a main dish or 8 as an appetizer.

Creamed Corn (recipe follows)

1 ½ cups pancake mix (multigrain, available from the bulk bin)

2 eggs, beaten

1 cup 2% milk

2 tablespoons unsalted butter, divided

BBQ Slaw (recipe follows)

½ cup chives (to garnish)

Chipotle BBQ Sauce (page 226) (to garnish)

Mix the Creamed Corn, pancake mix, eggs, and milk until just combined—do not overmix. On a nonstick griddle over medium-low heat, melt about 1 teaspoon of the butter to ensure that your corn cake doesn't stick. Spoon about ⅓ cup of the batter onto the griddle. Cook for 4 minutes or until the top looks like it has set. Flip and cook another 2 minutes. Repeat until all the batter has been used.

To serve, heap a corn cake with about ½ cup of BBQ Slaw; garnish with chives and a touch more BBQ sauce. Eat it with a fork like a civilized person—or pick it up like a taco, as Jason instructed me on the show.

Makes about 12 corn cakes.

CREAMED CORN

1 tablespoon unsalted butter

1 cup white onion, diced

2 cups corn, cut away

from the cob) (about 2 large ears)

⅛ teaspoon nutmeg

Sea salt flakes and cracked black pepper (to taste)

½ cup heavy cream

Melt the butter in a large sauté pan over medium-high heat. Add the onion and sauté until translucent. Add the corn and cook until the sugar in the corn begins to caramelize and some of the kernels begin to brown, about 4 minutes. Add the nutmeg, salt, pepper, and cream. Allow to cool.

Makes 3 cups.

BBQ SLAW

5 cups cabbage, shredded

1 tablespoon Creole mustard

2 cloves garlic, minced

½ cup olive oil mayonnaise

1 cup Chipotle BBQ
Sauce (page 226)

Sea salt flakes and cracked
black pepper (to taste)

In a large bowl toss the cabbage, mustard, garlic, mayo, and BBQ sauce until well incorporated. Season with salt and pepper to taste. Place in the fridge until ready to use.

Makes 4 cups.

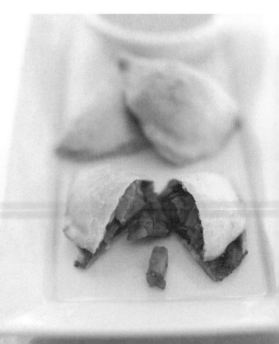

NATCHITOCHES UMAMI PIES WITH YOGURT CHIMICHURRI

We served this dish at our collaborative brunch at Chef Kelly English's Restaurant Iris in Memphis. We make our pies with black beans and pickled peppers. Kelly makes his with ground beef and allspice. Here, the combination of his spices and our filling work perfectly together. Even the sauce splits the difference between what he normally does at Iris and the sauce we typically serve in our home. We usually make a chunky chimichurri, and Kelly does a spicy buttermilk dip. Here is a creamy, yogurt-based chimichurri. We found a happy middle ground and a whole new dish when we combined our two styles.

1 ½ cups (1 can) prepared black beans

2 cups broth

1 teaspoon allspice

½ teaspoon dried thyme

½ teaspoon garlic powder

1 ½ tablespoons canola oil

1 cup finely diced onion (about half of 1 large)

½ cup finely diced celery (about 1 large rib)

½ cup white wine (like Pinot Grigio)

½ cup finely diced carrot (about 2 medium)

1 cup finely diced sweet potato (about 1 small)

¼ cup chopped pickled cherry peppers (4 to 5)

1 tablespoon soy sauce

1 teaspoon flour

Basic Piecrust Dough (page xx)

Egg wash (1 beaten egg mixed with 1 tablespoon water)

Yogurt Chimichurri (recipe follows)

½ teaspoon smoked paprika (for garnish)

Add the canola oil to a 12-inch frying pan over medium-high heat and sauté the onion and celery until translucent and beginning to brown. Deglaze the pan with the wine, and reduce until most of the liquid has evaporated. Add the carrot, potato, peppers, and soy sauce. Cook for 5 minutes, stirring frequently. Add the black beans. Sprinkle the flour over the mixture and stir to incorporate. This should tighten up any juices in the pan. Lightly mash half the mixture using a potato masher. Set the mixture aside to cool.

Preheat your oven to 350 degrees F. Roll the dough out on a floured surface to approximately a 16 x 12-inch rectangle. Using a drinking glass, cut as many circles from the dough as you can. Pick up a disk of dough, and place it into the palm of your hand. Spoon 1 to 1 ½ tablespoons of filling into the center of the round. Fold both ends up so it looks like a little taco. Pinch the open sides together with your fingers until sealed. Place on a parchment-lined baking sheet. Repeat until all dough has been used. Place in the oven for 20 minutes. Brush the tops with egg wash, and return the pies to the oven for another 15 to 20 minutes or until lightly browned.

To serve, place the pies on a serving platter alongside the Yogurt Chimichurri sauce and garnish with smoked paprika.

Makes 20 small pies.

YOGURT CHIMICHURRI

2 cups loose-packed parsley

1 medium clove garlic

Juice of 1 lemon (about
   1 tablespoon)

½ teaspoon cane sugar

2 teaspoons olive oil

¼ cup 2% Greek yogurt

½ teaspoon sea salt flakes

Cracked black pepper
(to taste)

Place the parsley, garlic, lemon juice, and sugar into the work bowl of your food processor. Drizzle in the olive oil slowly as the food processor runs. Stop the processor, and add the yogurt, salt, and pepper. Blend until very smooth. Pour into a small serving dish and place in the fridge until ready to serve.

Makes ½ cup.

SAMBAL PEPPER JELLY AND SAVORY CHEDDAR-PECAN COOKIES

This is inspired by two guilty pleasures here in the South: pepper jelly and cheese straws. These two items are ever-present at any gathering of merit. Pepper jelly is typically served with Cheddar on plain crackers, while cheese straws are just for snacking. This is a beautiful marriage of the two.

This pepper jelly is different from most you'll find around the South since a couple of ingredients, rice vinegar and sambal, sriracha's chunkier cousin, are borrowed from Asia. Another twist is using the natural pectin present in citrus peel as a gelling agent for this concoction.

This recipe serves 6–8 as an appetizer. Offer this at your next gathering, and your guests will think you're the sweetest thing they've ever seen.

SAMBAL PEPPER JELLY

1 cup cane sugar

¼ cup rice vinegar

½ cup minced red bell pepper (1 small)

1 tablespoon sambal

Peel of 1 lemon (use a vegetable peeler)

Place the sugar, vinegar, red pepper, sambal, and lemon peel in a small saucepan over low heat. Stir constantly as you gradually increase the heat until you bring the mixture to a boil. Continue to stir as it boils for 2 minutes. Pour the mixture into a half-pint jar. Stir occasionally to distribute the chopped pepper as it all starts to cool and gel. Keep refrigerated for up to a month.

Makes a half-pint.

SAVORY CHEDDAR-PECAN COOKIES

1 cup toasted pecans

1 cup all-purpose flour

¼ teaspoon hickory smoked salt

¼ teaspoon cracked black pepper

1 cup shredded sharp Cheddar cheese

2 tablespoons unsalted butter

4 tablespoons water

Place the pecans, flour, smoked salt, and black pepper in the work bowl of your food processor. Turn it on and let it run until the pecans and flour are indistinguishable from one another. Add the Cheddar and butter and turn it on again. Drizzle in the water one tablespoon at a time until the dough forms a ball and rolls around inside the work bowl. (You may not need all the water.)

continued next page ▸

On your work surface roll the dough into about a 7-inch log. Place the log on a plate in the freezer for 30 minutes to harden so you can slice it. While it's in the freezer, preheat your oven to 350 degrees F. Remove the dough and slice into ¼-inch slices. Place on a 17 x 12-inch parchment-lined baking sheet. Bake for 25 minutes or until lightly browned. Transfer the cookies to a plate or cooling rack and allow to cool before serving.

Makes about 24 savory cookies.

BBQ TOFU NACHOS WITH CHIPOTLE PINTO BEANS AND GUACAMOLE

We call it "Memphis veggie fusion"; it's when Memphis's BBQ culture collides with vegetarian cuisine. The result of this phenomenon is served up in restaurants, bars, and BBQ joints all around the city.

The Big Bang of Memphis veggie fusion happened in the mid-1990s at a little place near the University of Memphis called R.P. Trax. That's when our good buddy Chris Hawkins helped create R.P. Trax's original vegetarian menu. Today you can sit down and order BBQ tofu quesadillas with smoked gouda, a BBQ tofu sandwich with sweet potato fries, tofu wings with bleu cheese, or a BBQ tofu burrito. For brunch, they even have a breakfast burrito with scrambled eggs, and—you guessed it—BBQ tofu. Our all-time favorite is a Memphis original: BBQ tofu nachos. Imagine house-made chips with a cool ranch seasoning, vegetarian black bean chili, lettuce, tomato, pickled peppers, melted Cheddar, deep-fried BBQ tofu, and sour cream all piled onto a metal plate the size of your head. Two people could share this and walk away completely satisfied.

1 block extra-firm tofu

¼ cup canola oil

1 ½ cups Chipotle BBQ Sauce (page 226)

3 handfuls of corn tortilla chips (about half an 8-ounce bag)

2 cups Chipotle Pinto Beans (recipe follows)

½ cup shredded Cheddar cheese

1 ½ cups shredded iceberg lettuce

½ cup chopped tomatoes

½ cup No-Fuss Guacamole (recipe follows)

Cilantro leaves, sliced jalapeño peppers, and lime wedges (to garnish)

Start by making the panfried BBQ tofu. Cut the tofu into 1/2-inch cubes, and blot the excess water from it with a kitchen towel. Heat a large frying pan over high heat and add the oil. Once the oil starts to shimmer, brown the tofu on all sides in the pan. This takes only 2 minutes. Drain off any excess oil. Toss the cubes in warm BBQ sauce. Keep the tofu warm on the stovetop until you're ready to assemble the nachos.

Grab a large plate and start piling on the ingredients; start with the chips. Then add the beans, tofu, cheese, lettuce, tomatoes, and guacamole. Garnish with cilantro, jalapeño, and lime.

Serves 4 as an appetizer or 2 as a meal.

CHIPOTLE PINTO BEANS

1 tablespoon olive oil

1 cup diced white onion

¼ teaspoon dried chipotle chili powder

¼ teaspoon cumin

1 ½ cups prepared pinto beans (16-ounce can, drained)

1 cup chopped tomatoes (about 1 medium)

½ cup vegetable stock

½ teaspoon white vinegar

Sea salt flakes (to taste)

Add the olive oil to a medium pot over medium-high heat. Sauté the onion until translucent and just starting to brown. Add the chipotle and cumin and cook another minute. Add the beans, tomatoes, stock, and vinegar to the pot, and bring it to a boil. Simmer for 20 minutes or until the beans are creamy and the tomatoes have broken down. Salt to taste.

Makes 2 cups.

NO-FUSS GUACAMOLE

2 ripe Haas avocados

2 tablespoons finely diced red onion

Juice of ½ lime

¼ teaspoon sea salt flakes

⅛ teaspoon cane sugar

¼ teaspoon cracked black pepper

Peel and dice the avocados and place them in a medium bowl. Rinse the chopped onion in cold water to get rid of any astringent onion flavor. Add the lime juice, onion, salt, sugar, and black pepper and stir. Keep in the fridge (with the pit nestled into the guacamole in order to prevent browning) until ready to use.

Makes 1 cup.

GREEN PEA HUMMUS

Our sister-in-law makes green pea hummus for lots of get-togethers. It is so addictive that we had to give it a shot too! It's different from regular chickpea hummus because it has both a sweetness and a brightness that really shine.

4 tablespoons olive oil

1 ¼ teaspoons cumin

1 ¼ teaspoons coriander

3 cloves garlic, sliced

1 (16-ounce) bag of organic frozen green peas, defrosted

Zest of 1 lemon

¾ cup loose-packed fresh parsley

Sea salt flakes and cracked black pepper (to taste)

Pour the olive oil in a skillet over medium heat. Add the cumin and coriander and toast until fragrant. Add the garlic to the skillet. Cook this for a minute, but watch the garlic so that it doesn't burn! Add the spice mixture, peas, lemon zest, parsley, salt, and pepper to the food processor. Pulse until all the peas are thoroughly broken down and the mixture has the consistency of hummus. Serve with olive oil–fried toast (thin slices of baguette panfried in a little olive oil), whole wheat tortillas, or pita chips.

Makes 4 servings.

OKRA FRITTERS WITH CREOLE MUSTARD SAUCE

These fritters don't have any of the sliminess that sometimes turns people away from okra. How do we know this? After she proclaimed, "I don't eat green things," we watched our five-year-old niece try these okra fritters and exclaim, "I love okra!" Now that's a victory.

You can serve these any number of ways. They're great as a salad on a bed of arugula that's been dressed with our Creole Mustard Sauce and topped with fresh dill, parsley, and chopped tomatoes. They're also great as an okra po' boy slider on a French roll with lettuce, tomato, and dill. Or you can just dip the fritters right into the Creole Mustard Sauce as a simple appetizer.

1 tablespoon unsalted butter

½ cup finely diced white onion

2 cups sliced okra (¼-inch pieces, stem ends discarded)

⅛ teaspoon garlic powder

Scant ⅛ teaspoon nutmeg

⅛ teaspoon paprika

⅛ teaspoon sea salt flakes

⅛ teaspoon cracked black pepper

3 dashes hot sauce

2 tablespoons finely chopped parsley

¼ cup all-purpose flour

2 tablespoons yellow cornmeal

1 egg, beaten

Canola oil for frying

Creole Mustard Sauce (recipe follows)

In a 10-inch frying pan over medium heat, melt the butter and sauté the onion until translucent, about 3 minutes. In a large bowl mix together the sautéed onion, okra, garlic powder, nutmeg, paprika, salt, pepper, hot sauce, parsley, flour, cornmeal, and egg until well incorporated.

Heat ½ inch of canola oil in a 10-inch frying pan over medium heat. You may use the same pan as you used to sauté the onion. Once the oil shimmers, you are ready to add the okra mixture. Using an ice-cream scoop, place a ¼-cup portion of the okra mixture into the oil. Cook four fitters at a time for 1 to 2 minutes per side until golden brown. Drain on paper towels. Repeat until all the mixture has been used. Serve with Creole Mustard Sauce for dipping.

Makes 8 to 10 fritters.

CREOLE MUSTARD SAUCE

2 tablespoons mayonnaise

2 tablespoons Creole mustard

1 teaspoon ketchup

Juice of 1 lemon (about a teaspoon)

⅛ teaspoon sea salt flakes

Cracked black pepper (to taste)

Mix the mayonnaise, mustard, ketchup, lemon juice, salt, and pepper together in a small bowl. Keep in the refrigerator until you're ready to assemble the sandwiches.

Makes ½ cup.

OYSTER MUSHROOM ROCKEFELLER

This genius little dish was dreamed up by our good friend Michael Hughes. He did a version of it when he was the chef of a supper club dinner that we were lucky enough to attend.

We love the play on words: oyster mushrooms stand in for oysters in this Rockefeller. Besides that, it tastes really great, and they're fun to eat. The rich spinach bumps up against the meaty mushroom. The whole thing is topped with a crunchy Parmesan and bread crumb topping.

Oyster mushrooms can be found at many natural food markets and specialty grocery stores. However, to get the biggest and best (and the least expensive) mushrooms, seek out your local Asian foods market. You can substitute shiitake mushrooms if oyster mushrooms are not available.

Special equipment: 12 ceramic spoons*

2 tablespoons unsalted butter, divided

1 tablespoon olive oil (more for drizzling)

12 large oyster mushroom caps, woody stems trimmed off

Sea salt and cracked black pepper (to taste)

¼ cup diced shallots

1 tablespoon minced garlic

2 teaspoons Pernod (available at most liquor stores)

1 tablespoon vermouth

1 tablespoon all-purpose flour

½ cup whole milk

5 ounces fresh spinach, blanched, squeezed dry, and chopped

Sea salt flakes and cracked black pepper (to taste)

½ cup shredded Parmesan cheese

1 tablespoon bread crumbs

Lemon wedges (to garnish)

2 tablespoons finely chopped parsley (to garnish)

In a 12-inch frying pan over medium heat, melt 1 tablespoon of the butter and add the olive oil. Once the oil has come up to temperature, sear the mushroom caps until lightly browned on both sides. This should take 2 minutes per side. Remove the mushrooms from the pan and set them aside on a separate plate. Season them with salt and pepper to taste.

Into the same pan, along with any remaining oil and butter left in the pan, add the shallots and garlic. Cook for 3 minutes until the shallots are soft. Be sure to keep the mixture moving so the garlic does not burn. Add the Pernod and vermouth to the pan. Once the alcohol has evaporated, remove the shallot and garlic mixture and set aside in a separate bowl.

Melt the remaining 1 tablespoon of butter in the pan. Add the flour and whisk until fragrant, about 2 minutes. Whisk in the milk, making sure there are no lumps. Once the mixture starts to thicken, add the spinach and the garlic and shallot mixture. Add salt and pepper to taste.

continued next page ▶

Mix the Parmesan and bread crumbs together in a small bowl. Turn your oven on medium broil. You are now ready to assemble the dish. Gather 12 ceramic soup spoons. Place 1 tablespoon of the spinach mixture into each, 1 large oyster mushroom cap, 1 tablespoon of the Parmesan mixture, and a drizzle of olive oil. Broil for 4 minutes or until browned. Keep warm in a low oven until ready to serve. Serve garnished with lemon wedges and chopped parsley.

Makes 12. Serves 2 to 4.

*If ceramic spoons are not available, serve on crostini or small rounds of buttered, toasted bread.

Mini Potato and Buttermilk Pancakes with Beluga Lentils and Crème Fraîche (page 46)

MINI POTATO AND BUTTERMILK PANCAKES WITH BELUGA LENTILS AND CRÈME FRAÎCHE

Here, beluga lentils stand in for beluga caviar in this classic Russian dish. Our potato pancakes are tender and light, so they make a great canvas for the other flavors.

The beluga lentils are flavored with kombu, which is dried seaweed. It tastes exactly like the sea. Kombu, along with the sea salt, is fairly convincing. If you can't get beluga lentils, green lentils will work just fine.

This recipe will serve 6 as an appetizer, so it's a great dish for your holiday party—or just serve it along with a salad for a light meal.

1 ½ cups roughly chopped potato (about 1 medium one, peeled)

1 teaspoon water

1 tablespoon unsalted butter

½ cup all-purpose flour

1 package Rapid-Rise yeast

½ teaspoon sea salt flakes

1 teaspoon cane sugar

1 egg, beaten

1 cup buttermilk

Canola oil

½ cup crème fraîche, divided

Beluga Lentils (recipe follows)

4 sprigs fresh dill (to garnish)

Sea salt flakes and cracked black pepper (to taste)

Place the potato, water, and butter in a covered, microwave-safe dish and microwave on high for 6 minutes. In the meantime, mix the flour, yeast, salt, and sugar in a large bowl. In a small bowl, mix the egg and buttermilk. Run the potato through a ricer or mash thoroughly with a potato masher and place it into the large bowl with the flour. With a whisk mix the egg mixture with the flour mixture.

Cover the mixture and set aside for 30 minutes to allow it to rise. Adjust the thickness as needed using up to ¼ cup of water. (You want it to be as thick as pancake batter.)

In a 12-inch skillet over medium heat, heat 1 tablespoon of oil. Once the oil starts to shimmer, add the batter a tablespoon at a time to form small pancakes, called blini. (You will fit about five pancakes in the pan at a time.) Allow the blini to cook for 2 minutes per side. Cook in batches, and add a tablespoon of oil to the pan if the mixture looks dry.

To assemble the dish, top each blin with 1 teaspoon of crème fraîche followed by 1 teaspoon of Beluga Lentils. Garnish each with fresh dill, salt, and pepper.

Makes 24 blini.

BELUGA LENTILS

2 cups water

2 pieces kombu (dried
   seaweed)

½ cup black beluga lentils

1 tablespoon sea salt flakes

1 ½ tablespoons olive oil

Add the water, kombu, lentils, and salt to a saucepan. Bring it up to a boil and then allow it to simmer, covered, for 20 minutes or until tender. Allow the lentils to cool in the liquid. Remove the kombu and discard. Drain the lentils and then add the olive oil. Serve at room temperature.

Makes 1 cup.

TOFU AND TRUFFLE "PORK" RINDS

Sometimes we buy ingredients that we have no idea how to use until we experiment with them at home. That was the case with these frozen bean curd sheets we found at the Vietnamese market. Once we got them home, we figured fried tofu skins might puff up like pork rinds—and they did! To season them, we used some black truffle salt because everyone knows that truffles are the bacon of the future.

Enjoy these warm or at room temperature. They're good on their own or as an addition to cornbread or greens.

1 ½ cups canola oil

1 (9-ounce) package bean curd sheets (defrosted) or wonton wrappers

1 tablespoon black truffle salt

Pour a ¼-inch layer of canola oil in a 10-inch frying pan and set over medium heat. Tear the bean curd sheet into 2-inch strips. Fry one at a time, turning once. It will take only a few seconds for the skin to crisp. Drain on paper towels. Sprinkle each with a pinch or two of truffle salt to taste.

Makes 8 to 10 servings.

ZUCCHINI FRIES

We usually make these in the summer when there's more zucchini than we know what to do with coming out of the garden. What a great way to use up all of the overgrown zucchini—actually, the big guys are the best to use for this since they have much less water in 'em, and you can get so many cuts out of the seedless part. Make more than you think you'll need because you won't believe how much of these you'll want!

3 cups of peeled, matchstick-cut zucchini (about ½ inch thick and 4 inches long)

1 teaspoon sea salt

1 teaspoon Italian seasoning

½ cup all-purpose flour

1 egg, beaten

¼ cup whole milk

1 ½ cups coarse bread crumbs

¼ cup olive oil

1 tablespoon grated Parmesan cheese (for garnish)

Fresh parsley, finely chopped (for garnish)

Vegetable-Packed Tomato Sauce (page 229; for dipping)

Preheat the oven to 415 degrees F. In a large bowl sprinkle the zucchini fries with salt and Italian seasoning. Add the flour and toss to coat. Set up two stations, one with egg and whole milk whisked together in bowl and another separate bowl of bread crumbs. Dip each fry in the egg-and-milk mixture and then roll it in the bread crumbs. Place in a single layer on a parchment-lined baking sheet. Repeat until you've used all the zucchini. Drizzle the coated fries with olive oil. Bake for 20 minutes. Garnish with Parmesan and parsley and dip into tomato sauce.

Makes 4 servings.

SMOKED DATES STUFFED WITH GOAT CHEESE AND PECANS

We recently spent thirty dollars on an obsession, and it changed the way we cook. We bought a stainless steel hotel pan, a perforated pan, and a lid from a local kitchen supply store in order to make a vegetable smoking device. Why let the omnivores have all the fun with their smoky bacon and BBQ contests? We wanted to start smoking too.

Dates are one of my favorite foods to smoke. The sweetness of the date and the savoriness of the smoke play off of one another beautifully. Add some soft goat cheese and chopped pecans to make one perfect little bite. Think of this as the veg version of bacon-wrapped dates.

12 whole Medjool dates, smoked (Quick-Smoking Method on page 231)

2 ounces soft goat cheese, divided

½ cup chopped, toasted pecans, divided

Sea salt flakes and cracked black pepper (to taste)

2 tablespoons chopped chives (to garnish)

Using a sharp paring knife, split each date lengthwise, much the same as you would an avocado. Remove the pit and discard it. Next, roll ¼ teaspoon of the goat cheese between your fingers to form a tiny ball, and insert one goat cheese ball into the cavity of each date half. Add ¼ teaspoon of the chopped pecans to each half. Garnish with salt, pepper, and chopped chives.

Makes 24; serves 4 to 6.

SOUTHERN-STYLE CHEESE DIP

Here is an excerpt from our article "Cheese Dip Road Trip," which appeared in Edible Memphis:

According to In Queso Fever: A Movie about Cheese Dip, *cheese dip as we know it was invented in central Arkansas in the 1930s by an Irishman known as "Blackie" Donnelly, a guy who owned a restaurant called Mexico Chiquito. Wait . . . cheese dip was invented in Arkansas! So that makes cheese dip a Southern classic suitable to be served alongside cornbread and greens. That blew my mind when I first heard it.*

After all the research, we had to put our own spin on cheese dip by roasting fresh vegetables and leaving out the processed cheese. The result is what cheese dip would taste like in heaven. Make this recipe, which will serve 8 to 10 of your friends, for your next party.

1 large poblano pepper

1 medium jalapeño pepper

3 Roma tomatoes

¾ teaspoon cumin

1 teaspoon garlic powder

2 tablespoons unsalted butter

2 tablespoons all-purpose flour

1 cup buttermilk

¼ teaspoon sea salt flakes

Scant ⅛ teaspoon cayenne pepper

¼ pounds Oaxaca cheese, shredded (substitute mozzarella, if needed)

½ pound sharp Cheddar cheese, shredded

2 tablespoons chopped cilantro (to garnish; optional)

½ teaspoon minced red or green jalapeño (to garnish; optional)

1 bag white corn chips

Roast the peppers and tomatoes until blackened over a high flame on your outdoor grill; this should take 5 to 8 minutes. Place the peppers and tomatoes in a covered container and allow them to cool completely. Remove the stems and seeds from the peppers. Remove the core from the tomato using a paring knife. Slip the vegetables out of their charred skins.

Place the roasted vegetables, cumin, and garlic powder into the work bowl of your food processor. Pulse until the mixture is well incorporated. This process should yield about a cup of salsa.

In a 3-quart saucepan over medium heat, melt the butter and then whisk in the flour. Allow the flour and butter mixture to cook for 2 minutes until nutty and fragrant before whisking in the buttermilk. After about 2 minutes the mixture will thicken. Add the salt and cayenne. Add the cheese in batches, and stir the mixture so that the cheese melts completely. Once all the cheese is incorporated, add the homemade salsa and heat the mixture through.

Place everything back into the food processor and process for 3 minutes or until completely smooth. Pour the warm cheese dip into a serving bowl and garnish with the chopped cilantro and minced jalapeño. Serve warm alongside crunchy corn tortilla chips.

Refrigerate any unused portion (as if there will be any left over!). Reheat in the microwave for a minute and a half or in a saucepan on low heat.

Makes about 1 ½ pints.

HOPPIN' JOHN BLACK-EYED PEA BUTTER

Don't save the black-eyed peas for New Year's Day. This is a super-easy treat you can enjoy all year long. This dish splits the difference between traditional hummus and Southern American fare, but the outcome is something very special. The creaminess of the peas serves as the perfect vehicle for the heat of the hot sauce and the smokiness of the salt.

This is a great dish for a party. You can make it ahead of time and have it on the table when your ravenous guests arrive. For a little extra flair, save a few peas to garnish the top of the dish.

1 tablespoon olive oil

2 large garlic cloves, smashed

½ teaspoon coriander

¼ teaspoon cumin

1 ½ cups prepared black-eyed peas (or 1 can drained)

½ teaspoon hot sauce

Juice of ½ lemon (about 1 teaspoon)

1 tablespoon tahini

½ teaspoon hickory-smoked sea salt

¼ teaspoon cracked black pepper

In a medium pan over medium-low heat, add the olive oil, garlic, coriander, and cumin. Cook for about 5 minutes or until the garlic has softened. Add the contents of the pan to the work bowl of your food processor along with the black-eyed peas, hot sauce, lemon juice, tahini, hickory-smoked sea salt, and pepper. Blend until smooth. Serve with toasted baguette or pita chips.

Makes 1 ½ cups; serves 4.

DEVILED EGG AND OLIVE

Egg and olive together is one of those uniquely Southern combinations. We love egg and olive sandwiches for leisurely Saturday lunches, and here, we decided to include those same flavors into a deviled egg. The result is a punchy, salty, rich kick in the tastebuds.

6 large eggs

1 cup distilled white vinegar

¼ cup iodized salt

2 teaspoons Creole mustard

2 tablespoons olive
   oil mayonnaise

¼ teaspoon red pepper flakes

¼ cup chopped celery (1 rib)

¼ cup thinly sliced
   green olives (about 8,
   more for garnish)

Sweet paprika (to garnish)

Fresh dill (to garnish)

Cracked black pepper
   (to taste)

Start by hard-boiling the eggs. First, add the eggs to a cold, medium pot. Next, pour in the white vinegar and then the salt and enough water to cover the eggs by 1 inch. Over high heat bring the contents to a boil. Once the water is boiling rapidly, turn the heat off and cover. Leave the eggs in the hot water for 10 minutes. Remove the eggs to an ice bath and allow them to chill completely. Roll each egg under your palm on a cutting board to fracture the shell completely. Under cold running water, pick the shell off one piece at a time until the egg slips out of the shell.

Once you've peeled all the eggs, use a sharp knife to cut the hard-boiled eggs in half longways. Carefully push the yolk out of the center of each egg into the work bowl of a food processor. Set the egg whites aside in the refrigerator until the filling is ready. Add the mustard, mayonnaise, red pepper flakes, and celery to the yolks. Blend until smooth. In a small bowl mix the yolk mixture with the sliced olives.

Using a small ice-cream scoop, scoop 1 tablespoon of the mixture into the center of each egg white. Garnish with a small sprinkling of sweet paprika, a thinly sliced green olive, a sprig of dill, and cracked black pepper.

Makes 12; serves 4.

GRILLED WATERMELON AND TOMATO SALAD WITH HONEY-LIME VINAIGRETTE

It's amazing how some foods can be transformed once they've been grilled. Take watermelon, for instance. We think of it as being sweet like a dessert that's perfect to cool us down during the hot Southern summer. But add a little heat from the grill and some more heat from chili powder, and the watermelon slices go from sweet to savory.

- 1 personal-size watermelon (smaller than a volleyball)
- 2 medium yellow tomatoes, sliced ¼ inch thick
- 2 cups halved cherry tomatoes
- 4 ounces soft goat cheese
- Honey-Lime Vinaigrette (recipe follows)
- 1 teaspoon ancho chili powder, divided
- ½ teaspoon sea salt flakes, divided
- 1 cup loose-packed cilantro leaves (to garnish)

Preheat your outdoor grill to high. Cut two 1-inch-thick slices from the heart of the watermelon. Then cut the slices into quarters. Grill one side of the watermelon slices until the sugar starts to caramelize. The watermelon should be well-marked by the grill grates. Remove from the grill and set aside. Do not flip and grill the other side because the watermelon will fall apart.

To serve, place 1 to 2 slices of yellow tomato on the serving plate, and top that with 1 to 2 slices of the grilled watermelon, ¼ cup of the halved cherry tomatoes, and 1 ounce of the soft goat cheese. Drizzle 1 tablespoon of the Honey-Lime Vinaigrette over the dish, sprinkle with ¼ teaspoon of ancho chili powder, and salt to taste. Finish the dish with a few fresh cilantro leaves. Repeat the process for each serving.

Makes 4 servings.

HONEY-LIME VINAIGRETTE

- Juice of 1 lime (about 2 tablespoons)
- Zest of 1 lime
- 2 tablespoons honey
- 2 tablespoons olive oil
- Scant ⅛ teaspoon cayenne pepper

Place the lime juice, zest, honey, olive oil, and cayenne in a small jar with a lid and then shake the jar until the dressing emulsifies. Set aside until ready to use.

Makes about ⅓ cup.

SOUTHERN CAESAR SALAD WITH CORNBREAD CROUTONS

For quite some time, this dish was just a hasty idea scrawled on a piece of paper, along with notes that read stuffed hush puppies, boiled peanuts, and Carolina Gold arancini. We'll get around to those other ideas eventually, but we sure are glad we tackled this particular dish first. The Creole mustard and the cornbread take this salad way down South for a trip you're not likely to forget, especially if you make it using our Smoked Cheddar Jalapeño Cornbread (page 153).

4 cups cubed smoked Cheddar Jalapeño Cornbread (page 153)

Juice of ½ lemon (about 1 tablespoon)

½ teaspoon Creole mustard

2 tablespoons olive oil mayonnaise

1 medium garlic clove, minced

1 teaspoon vegetarian Worcestershire sauce

1 teaspoon honey

Cracked black pepper (to taste)

6 cups chopped romaine lettuce (about 7 ounces)

½ cup grated Parmesan cheese (to garnish)

Preheat your oven to 350 degrees F. Place the cornbread cubes on a parchment-lined sheet pan in a single layer. Bake for 15 minutes or until golden brown. Set croutons aside to cool. In a large bowl whisk together the lemon juice, mustard, mayonnaise, garlic, Worcestershire sauce, honey, and pepper. Using tongs, toss the romaine lettuce and the cornbread croutons in the dressing. Divide among plates and garnish with Parmesan.

Makes 2 large or 4 small salads.

SUMMER SALAD

My grandma used to make this concoction out of tomatoes, cucumber, onions, vinegar, sugar, salt, and water. She kept it in a seafoam-green plastic container in the fridge, and I got in a ton of trouble once it became obvious that I was the one secretly picking out all the tomatoes. Biee, as we called her, would ask where all the tomatoes went, and I would shrug. But I knew she knew.

Think of this summer salad as you would a quick pickle. Leave it overnight or store it in the fridge for about a week. Strain the salad and serve it with a drizzle of olive oil. It's summer simplicity and perfection on a plate.

2 cucumbers, sliced (about 3 cups)

2 medium tomatoes, sliced and quartered (about 2 cups)

1 small white onion, thinly sliced (about 1 cup)

1 cup white vinegar

1 ½ cups water

1 tablespoon sea salt flakes

¼ cup cane sugar

Slice the cucumber any way you'd like. The easiest way is to slice it into "coins," but it's also fine to slice it longways using a vegetable peeler. Place the sliced cucumber, tomatoes, onion, vinegar, water, salt, and sugar in a 2-quart food storage container. Stir and then refrigerate for a day before serving.

Makes 4 to 6 salads.

ROAST BEET SALAD WITH SEA SALT GRANOLA AND HONEY-TARRAGON DRESSING

The addition of granola to a salad may seem unusual, but its nutty flavor and crunchy texture are right at home atop sliced beets and goat cheese. Don't be deterred by the amount of steps as it's really quite simple to put together. Just make the beets ahead of time since they need to cook for an hour and a half.

- 5 medium red beets
- ½ cup white wine (like Pinot Grigio)
- 4 cloves garlic, smashed
- 2 tablespoons soy sauce
- 8 sprigs thyme
- ¼ teaspoon cracked black pepper
- ¼ teaspoon sea salt flakes
- 2 tablespoons olive oil
- ½ cup Sea Salt Granola (page 232)
- Honey Tarragon Dressing (recipe follows)
- 4 cups lettuce (Boston or baby romaine)
- 4 ounces soft goat cheese, crumbled

Preheat your oven to 350 degrees F. Trim ⅛ inch from both the stem end and the root end of each beet. Place the beets in a small casserole dish, along with the wine, garlic cloves, soy sauce, thyme, pepper, salt, and olive oil. Cover tightly with aluminum foil and bake for 1 ½ hours.

Allow the beets to cool completely. Peel the skin from each beet by rubbing it with a damp paper towel just as though you're polishing it—the outer skin will rub right off. Slice the beets into ¼-inch sections. Discard the cooking liquid.

Follow the directions below to make the granola and dressing. The beets and the dressing are proportioned correctly for this recipe, but the granola will make more than you need for this dish.

Once your components are made, all that's left to do is assemble the salad. Start by layering beets and lettuce together like you would a caprese salad. Each serving should get 5 to 6 slices of beet. Next, drizzle the assemblage with about a tablespoon of the Honey Tarragon Dressing. Finish with an ounce of crumbled goat cheese and ⅛ cup of Sea Salt Granola.

Makes 4 servings.

HONEY-TARRAGON DRESSING

- Juice of 1 lemon (about 1 tablespoon)
- 1 tablespoon honey
- ½ teaspoon minced tarragon
- ½ teaspoon minced chives
- ¼ teaspoon sea salt flakes
- ¼ teaspoon cracked black pepper
- ¼ cup olive oil

In a small bowl add the lemon juice, honey, tarragon, chives, salt, and pepper together. Drizzle the olive oil into the mixture as you whisk to emulsify the dressing. Set the mixture aside.

Makes ½ cup.

WARM BRUSSELS SPROUT SALAD WITH SMOKED FETA AND CANDIED PECANS

A number of people in our family have fallen for the vegetable that is often the butt of the joke: the humble Brussels sprout. It's all due to this salad. This dish has it all: sweet, savory, smoky, and rich flavors. Without fail, it's the one dish everyone requests that we make at Thanksgiving.

1 pound Brussels sprouts (15 to 20 larger ones work best here)

¼ cup cane sugar

1 ½ cups whole roasted and salted pecans

4 ounces smoked feta*

4 tablespoons olive oil

2 tablespoons golden balsamic vinegar (or champagne vinegar)

Sea salt flakes and cracked black pepper (to taste)

Start by tearing apart the Brussels sprouts. Cut off about ⅓ of the stem end and pull the leaves apart. This takes some time, but it's worth it. Start by pressing outward with your thumbs on the cut side. This will yield the largest leaves and make for a fluffier salad. Blanch the leaves in boiling, salted water (as salty as the sea) until they turn bright green. This will take 10 seconds. Run the leaves under cold water to stop the cooking. Dry the sprout leaves in a salad spinner or lay them out on a clean towel to dry.

Spread the sugar in a cold 10-inch frying pan and melt over medium heat. Once the edges of the sugar start to melt, stir the sugar until all the lumps disappear. Remove from the heat. Toss the pecans in the melted sugar until coated. It will look a bit like spun sugar as you stir the pecans into the sugar, and the pecans will stick together as they cool. Transfer to a plate to cool completely. Once the pecans have cooled, break the mass apart using your hands and give them a rough chop. Cut the feta into a ¼-inch dice.

Now you're ready to assemble the salad. Place olive oil and vinegar into a large frying pan over low heat. The heat should not be so high that the dressing sizzles. Once the dressing is warm, place the sprout leaves in the pan and toss with the dressing. Transfer to a large plate. Sprinkle with cheese and nuts; add salt and pepper to taste.

Makes 4 servings.

*If you cannot find smoked feta in your area, just use feta cheese and add ¼ teaspoon Liquid Smoke to the dressing. The result will be much the same.

CAPRESE SALAD IN A JAR

One day we brought home the ingredients for caprese salad; of course, we just couldn't leave well enough alone. This salad-in-jars recipe is basic, but the results are pretty and fun; may the ridiculous appeal of serving all sorts of food in jars live on for many salads to come! Using small ingredients, cherry tomatoes and mini bocconcini, creates a cute effect.

Special equipment: 4 medium-sized wide-mouth jars with lids

½ cup loose-packed green basil leaves

½ cup loose-packed purple basil leaves

2 cups baby arugula

1 cup halved cherry tomatoes

8 ounces mini bocconcini

Balsamic Vinaigrette (recipe follows)

Tear the larger basil leaves and leave the smaller ones whole. One ingredient at a time, layer first the arugula, then the basils, tomatoes, and bocconcini into 4 jars. Set the open jars in the fridge to chill. When you're ready to serve the salads, drizzle the dressing on top of the salad, close the lids, and tell whoever's eating the salad to shake it up to mix everything together. Enjoy the salad straight from the jar.

Makes 4 servings.

BALSAMIC VINAIGRETTE

2 tablespoons olive oil

½ tablespoon balsamic vinegar

⅛ teaspoon honey

⅛ teaspoon sea salt flakes

⅛ teaspoon cracked black pepper

Whisk together the olive oil, vinegar, honey, salt, and pepper. Set aside in a container and shake to emulsify before drizzling over the salad.

Makes ¼ cup.

COLLARD GREENS (OR ANY GREENS!) WITH HONEY, SHALLOTS, AND MUSHROOMS

Vicky, a checker at the grocery store next door to our old apartment, shared this tip with us: Whenever you're making greens, drizzle a little honey in the pot. It'll take away any lingering bitterness. It worked perfectly the very first time, so we've been making greens with a little drizzle of honey for more than ten years now.

This particular recipe calls for collard greens, but you could use any hearty greens you like. In fact, we like using a mix of kale, mustard, and collards best. Unlike many Southerners, we don't cook our greens until they are mush. This way, they're vibrant and tasty.

4 quarts water

¼ cup iodized salt

2 bunches collards (6 to 8 cups when trimmed)

1 ½ tablespoons canola oil

1 ½ cups sliced button mushrooms

1 cup sliced shallot

¼ teaspoon cracked black pepper

¼ teaspoon hickory smoked sea salt

¼ teaspoon garlic powder

1 teaspoon honey

In an 8-quart stock pot bring the water and salt up to a boil. Use a paring knife to trim the leaves of the greens away from the tough stems—simply run your knife along the stem. Roll leaves and trim into half-inch ribbons. You should have 6 to 8 cups of leaves once the greens are trimmed and sliced. Blanch the leaves in salt water for 2 minutes or until the leaves turn bright green. Remove the leaves from the water into a colander to drain. Carefully discard the water down the drain; run a little cold water while you pour the hot water out so you don't damage your plumbing.

Return the pot to the burner. Over high heat add the canola oil and then the mushrooms in a single layer in the bottom of the pan. Allow the mushrooms to cook undisturbed for 3 minutes or until they get some color on them. Turn the heat to low. Add the shallot, pepper, smoked salt, and garlic powder. Sauté until fragrant (about 1 minute). Add the collard greens and drizzle in the honey. Toss the greens with tongs to incorporate all the ingredients. Cover and keep the greens warm over very low heat until you're ready to serve them.

Makes 4 servings.

SOUPS AND SANDWICHES

Vegetarian "Midnight Snack" Inspired by Restaurant Iris   77

Crispy Eggplant Sandwiches and Roasted Garlic and Ricotta Spread   79

Smoked Coconut Bacon   82

Lemon Zest and Thyme Pimento Cheese   84

Fried Chickpea Sandwich with Blue Cheese and Tomato   86

Fried Green Tomato Po' Boy   88

BBQ Portobello Mushroom Sandwich with Smoked Gouda   91

Vegetarian Roasted Red Pepper and Olive Muffuletta   92

Simple and Easy Porcini Mushroom Veggie Burgers   94

Vegan Sloppy Joes   97

Smoky Grilled Vegetable Quesadillas   99

Triple Tomato Soup with Toasted White Cheddar Crouton   100

Curried Cauliflower Soup   102

Saffron Egg Drop Soup   105

Watermelon and Tomato Gazpacho   106

Mexican Corn Chowder   108

The Chubby Vegetarian Gumbo   111

Vegetarian Frogmore Stew   114

VEGETARIAN "MIDNIGHT SNACK" INSPIRED BY RESTAURANT IRIS

A few years ago in the kitchen of Restaurant Iris, I watched Chef Kelly English prepare his dish Midnight Snack for a photo shoot. It's made with toasted brioche, a poached egg, and sautéed shrimp that are tossed in his signature rémoulade sauce. I told him right then and there that I was going to make a vegetarian version of that dish. I did—and it was awesome.

Recently, Kelly kindly sent me the recipe for his rémoulade sauce. I made the dish again with his recipe, and it was quite a revelation. His rémoulade is so punchy and flavorful because of the addition of horseradish and sherry vinegar. He balances it out with a touch of sugar. It's just perfect.

1 tablespoon iodized salt

¼ cup white vinegar

4 large eggs

1 tablespoon unsalted butter, softened

4 1-inch thick slices of brioche bread

1 tablespoon canola oil, divided

2 ½ cups quartered mushrooms (10 ounces)

1 ½ cups quartered artichoke hearts (prepare your own or use 1 can)

Chef Kelly English's Rémoulade Sauce (recipe follows)

4 sprigs fresh dill (to garnish)

Cracked black pepper and sea salt flakes (to taste)

In a large pan over medium heat, bring an inch and a half of water to a simmer. Add the salt and vinegar to the water and return it to a simmer. Poach 4 eggs at a time by slowly cracking the egg into the simmering water and allowing it to cook for 4 to 5 minutes or until the white is set. Remove the eggs from the water and set them aside on a paper towel until ready to serve. Discard the cooking water.

Spread butter onto the slices of brioche. Using the same pan as you did for the eggs, toast the slices of brioche over medium heat just as you would a grilled cheese sandwich. Once the bread has achieved a light brown color, remove it from the pan.

Again using the same pan, crank the heat up to high. Add ½ tablespoon canola oil to the pan. Once the oil starts smoking, add the mushrooms and cook for 3 minutes. Remove them from the pan. Add the remaining canola oil to the pan, along with the artichoke hearts. Cook for 3 minutes or until the edges turn golden brown. Turn the heat off. Add the mushrooms back to the pan, along with Chef Kelly English's Rémoulade Sauce. Toss to coat.

Divide the mushrooms and artichoke mixture among the toasted brioche slices, top with a poached egg, and garnish with fresh dill, cracked black pepper, and sea salt to taste.

Makes 4 servings.

CHEF KELLY ENGLISH'S RÉMOULADE SAUCE

⅓ cup olive oil mayonnaise

¼ cup Creole mustard

Juice of ½ lemon

1 teaspoon sherry vinegar

½ teaspoon celery salt

¼ teaspoon cane sugar

½ teaspoon sweet paprika

¼ teaspoon onion powder

⅛ teaspoon granulated garlic

2 teaspoons prepared horseradish

1 teaspoon chopped chives

In a large bowl mix together the mayonnaise, mustard, lemon juice, vinegar, celery salt, sugar, paprika, onion powder, granulated garlic, horseradish, and chives until well incorporated. Keep in a food storage container in the refrigerator. Any extra sauce can be frozen for up to 4 months.

Makes ⅔ cup.

CRISPY EGGPLANT SANDWICHES AND ROASTED GARLIC AND RICOTTA SPREAD

Many days we eat sandwiches for breakfast or lunch, but this particular sandwich is hearty enough to have for supper. The key is to choose a good eggplant—the fresher the better. Look for a smooth skin and no soft spots. Here, we pair the crispy eggplant with arugula, tomato sauce, and roasted garlic ricotta spread.

3 cups torn fresh bread (ciabatta or French bread)

1 tablespoon Italian seasoning mix

1 medium eggplant (makes about 12 slices)

Sea salt flakes and cracked black pepper (to taste)

1 cup all-purpose flour (for dredging)

2 large eggs, beaten

2 ½ teaspoons olive oil, divided

4 ciabatta or sesame kaiser rolls

2 cups arugula

1 cup Vegetable-Packed Tomato Sauce (page 229)

½ cup shredded Parmesan cheese (more for garnish)

Roasted Garlic and Ricotta Spread (recipe follows)

Preheat your oven to 375 degrees F. Make bread crumbs from the fresh bread by adding the torn bread and the Italian seasoning to the work bowl of your food processor. Pulse until the bread has broken down into a fine crumb. Place bread crumbs in a medium bowl and set aside.

Slice the eggplant ¼- to ½ inch thick. Sprinkle each slice with salt and pepper to taste. Set up a line of three medium bowls. The first bowl should contain the flour, the second the eggs, and the third the bread crumbs. Dredge each eggplant slice in the flour, shake off the excess, dip the slice in the egg, and then roll it in the bread crumbs to coat. Arrange the eggplant slices on a large, parchment-lined baking sheet. Drizzle each with ⅛ teaspoon of olive oil and put them into the oven. After 15 minutes, flip the slices and drizzle each slice with more olive oil. Continue cooking for another 15 minutes.

Remove the eggplant and warm your bread in the oven. Assemble the sandwich like this: arugula, three slices of eggplant, ⅛ cup warm tomato sauce, and a sprinkle of Parmesan. Spread some Roasted Garlic and Ricotta Spread on the underside of the top bun.

Makes 4 sandwiches.

ROASTED GARLIC AND RICOTTA SPREAD

3 cloves garlic (in their papery skins)

1 cup whole milk ricotta cheese

¼ cup shredded Parmesan cheese

The fast way to roast garlic is to put the garlic cloves skin-on into a dry, hot skillet. Allow them to cook until the skin is blackened. Let them cool, and inside the burnt skin you'll find a soft, smoky, sweet clove of garlic.

Using a fork mix the ricotta, roasted garlic cloves, and Parmesan together in a small bowl.

Makes 1 ¼ cups.

Crispy Eggplant Sandwiches and Roasted
Garlic and Ricotta Spread (page 79)

SMOKED COCONUT BACON

On The Food Network's website, we watched a video of Chef Jesse Kimball of The Memphis Tap Room in Philadelphia, Pennsylvania, make this amazing-looking, crunchy, smoky, non-bacon bacon. We've been looking for a vegetable medium or process that'll have that crispy crunch like bacon, and this coconut idea is brilliant.

We emailed Chef Kimball out of the blue, and he was happy to share the recipe and talk about his food. Thanks to him, you too can whip up a batch using a bag of shaved coconut with soy sauce, vegetarian Worcestershire, and maple syrup added to the mix for that sweet, Southern, bacon-y flavor. The coconut takes the smoke beautifully, and when it's baked, the inherent fat in the coconut crisps the flakes. The best part is that they stay crispy. You can make a big batch of this and have it as part of your lunch all week.

We have used this many different ways since first making it: as a garnish for an omelet, on pesto flatbreads, and on top of grits. However, our favorite has to be this avocado BLT. All you do is load up two slices of seeded whole wheat bread with sliced heirloom tomatoes, olive oil mayonnaise, crunchy romaine, sliced avocado, and plenty of Smoked Coconut Bacon. It's beautiful to hear the crunch of the bacon when you slice the sandwich in half.

3 ½ cups unsweetened coconut flakes

2 tablespoons maple syrup

2 tablespoons soy sauce

1 teaspoon cracked black pepper

1 tablespoon vegetarian Worcestershire sauce

1 tablespoon sesame oil

1 tablespoon liquid smoke (only if you don't smoke the coconut on the grill top)

Smoke the coconut flakes for 4 minutes using our Quick-Smoking Method (page 231). (That doesn't sound like a long time, but the coconut really soaks up the smoke quickly. This ain't no pork belly, y'all!)

Preheat your oven to 350 degrees F. Place the smoked coconut in a large bowl, and add the maple syrup, soy sauce, pepper, Worcestershire, and sesame oil. (Only add the liquid smoke if you didn't smoke the coconut. This is just an option for people without access to a smoker.) Toss to coat. Spread the dressed coconut into a single layer on a parchment-lined 17 x 12-inch sheet pan or two smaller pans. Cook the coconut for 10 minutes, stir it around, spread it back out on the sheet pan, and cook it another 5 minutes or until it is nice and dark brown. Let it cool and then store it in an airtight container for up to a week.

Makes 3 ½ cups.

LEMON ZEST AND THYME PIMENTO CHEESE

Growing up, we thought everyone ate pimento cheese sandwiches, but we had no idea until recently that it's a Southern thing. The largest producer of pimentos is actually based in Tennessee! We love living in the South because there's an abundance of heart, soul, and pimento cheese.

Our version is spiced with plenty of fresh thyme, lemon zest, and shallots. We use a combination of sharp cheddar cheese and soft goat cheese to give this pimento cheese a tangy, up-front flavor.

1 organic lemon

1 teaspoon fresh thyme (4-6 sprigs)

½ pound sharp Cheddar cheese, shredded

4 ounces soft goat cheese

¼ cup olive oil mayonnaise

1 cup finely diced red bell pepper (about 1 medium)

¼ teaspoon champagne vinegar

1 tablespoon minced shallot*

¼ teaspoon cracked black pepper

Sea salt flakes (to taste)

Zest the lemon using a zester and pull leaves from the sprigs of thyme by running your pinched fingers down the stem. Mix the Cheddar, goat cheese, thyme, zest, mayonnaise, bell pepper, vinegar, shallot, black pepper, and salt until incorporated. For best results, refrigerate for at least an hour to allow the flavors to meld.

Serve on thick slices of rustic country bread with a few slices of summer tomato and arugula, or use it to stuff peppadew peppers for a great appetizer.

Makes about 2 cups, enough pimento cheese for 6 sandwiches or 24 stuffed peppers.

*Place the minced shallot into a mesh strainer and run it under cold water for a few seconds. This will take away any raw onion flavor and keep the shallot from overpowering the dish.

FRIED CHICKPEA SANDWICH WITH BLUE CHEESE AND TOMATO

In Sicily, they call these simple little chickpea fritters panelle, and they're typically served as street food on a bun with a scoop of ricotta. In this down-South version, the chickpea fritters stand in for fried chicken.

A little magic happens when these things begin to cook. The outside layer of the fritter becomes craggy and crispy, the next layer is slightly chewy, and the center is creamy. They are so good that they're worth a few extra calories.

2 cups chickpea flour

2 cups vegetable broth, chilled

½ cup water

1 tablespoon olive oil

2 cups canola oil (for frying)

Sea salt flakes and cracked black pepper (to taste)

6 soft sesame buns

¼ cup olive oil mayonnaise

2 cups fresh baby spinach (to garnish)

6 tomato slices (to garnish)

¼ cup thinly sliced shallot (to garnish)

4 ounces crumbled blue cheese (to garnish)

In a medium saucepan add the chickpea flour to the cold broth and whisk. Gradually bring the mixture up to a low boil as you whisk. Once the mixture thickens, add the water and whisk some more. Cover and allow the mixture to cook on low for 5 minutes while stirring occasionally so that the bottom of the pan doesn't scorch.

In an olive oil–coated 12 x 9-inch casserole dish, quickly spread the flour mixture evenly to the edges. Use a sheet of waxed paper to press the mixture into place. Set aside on the counter to cool.

Once the mixture has cooled completely, turn it out onto a cutting board. Cut it into 2-inch squares and then cut each square in half to form triangles. Heat the canola oil to 350 degrees F. Fry the chickpea patties in batches of five for 4 minutes or until their color passes golden brown to turn more of a toasted brown. Sprinkle each with salt and pepper to taste.

To serve, toast the buns, spread with a teaspoon of mayonnaise, pile on three or four fritters, a handful of spinach, a slice of tomato, a few sliced shallots, and a sprinkle of blue cheese.

Makes 6 sandwiches.

FRIED GREEN TOMATO PO' BOY

This fried green tomato po' boy is just right. The dredge has a hint of nutmeg, and the N'awlins Sauce puts it over the top—way over the top. When selecting the bread for this sandwich, look for a baguette that has a crunchy exterior and is light for its size, not one that is soft and chewy. French baguette should be available at most grocery stores or specialty stores. Not only is it more authentic, it's easier to eat.

2 cups canola oil (for frying)

1 egg, beaten

1 cup all-purpose flour

About 1 cup water (to make the batter as thick as pancake batter)

½ cup cornstarch

½ cup cornmeal

1 teaspoon sea salt

1 tablespoon sweet paprika

¼ teaspoon nutmeg

½ teaspoon garlic powder

Scant ⅛ teaspoon cayenne pepper (optional)

5 medium green tomatoes, sliced into ½-inch slices

1 3-foot-long crusty, French baguette

4 ounces soft goat cheese

N'awlins Sauce (recipe follows)

2 cups baby spinach

2 medium red tomatoes, sliced

½ cup sliced green onion (to garnish)

Sea salt flakes and cracked black pepper (to taste)

Pour the canola oil into a saucepan (the oil should be about 2 inches deep). Heat the oil to 350 degrees F. Make the batter by whisking together the egg, flour, and enough water in a medium bowl to make the mixture as thick as pancake batter. Now make the dredge by tossing the cornstarch, cornmeal, salt, paprika, nutmeg, garlic powder, and cayenne pepper together in a separate bowl. Using a pair of tongs, dip each green tomato slice into the batter and allow the excess to drip off, leaving a thick coating of batter on the tomato. Then sprinkle the dredge over the tomato, allowing the excess to go back into the bowl. Do this just before placing each tomato into the oil. Fry in batches for 5 minutes or until golden brown. Drain on paper towels.

To assemble the sandwich, slice a crusty French loaf in half but leave one long side intact—this hinge will help keep the sandwich together as you bite into it. Pull the bread out of the top half to create a channel for the ingredients. Spread creamy goat cheese on the bottom part of the inside and N'awlins Sauce on the top. Layer in fresh spinach, sliced red tomato, and the fried green tomatoes. Garnish with green onion, salt, and pepper. Slice into 6-inch sections.

Makes 4 sandwiches.

N'AWLINS SAUCE

¼ cup olive oil mayonnaise

2 tablespoons Creole mustard

1 teaspoon vegetarian Worcestershire

Hot sauce (to taste)

Mix the mayonnaise, mustard, Worcestershire, and hot sauce in a small bowl until well incorporated.

Makes ½ cup.

BBQ PORTOBELLO MUSHROOM SANDWICH WITH SMOKED GOUDA

The Blondises are good folk. They run Central BBQ here in Memphis, and it's a definite favorite of many Memphians. They serve their fair share of tourists, but that actual Memphis residents love this place is in itself a high honor. I always look forward to going there to eat BBQ since Central offers a stellar BBQ portobello sandwich that we vegetarians really appreciate!

Our buddy J.C., the manager at Central, was kind enough to share their recipe with us, so now you can make this amazing sandwich at home. It's perfect to make in the backyard this summer—especially if you expect to have a few vegetarians drop by. But there's nothing like sitting on the front porch at Central BBQ and enjoying this sandwich as hickory smoke wafts through the air.

They make their own Italian dressing at Central, and their house-made BBQ sauce is killer. I've simplified the recipe here so you can make this in a hurry and feed the masses.

6 large portobello mushroom caps, stems trimmed

1 (16-ounce) bottle Italian dressing

1 tablespoon Memphis BBQ Dry Rub (recipe on page 225)

6 large slices smoked Gouda (about ½ pound)

6 hamburger buns

½ cup BBQ sauce for serving (store-bought is fine for this at-home version)

BBQ Slaw (page 29)

Wipe the mushrooms with a damp cloth to clean them. Choose a bottle of Italian dressing that is emulsified, meaning that it doesn't separate in the bottle. Marinate the mushrooms by pouring the Italian dressing over them and placing them in a sealed container in the refrigerator for at least an hour or up to 24 hours.

Preheat your outdoor grill to high. Remove the mushrooms from the marinade and place them on a sheet pan. Sprinkle both sides of each mushroom with our Memphis BBQ Dry Rub seasoning. Grill the mushrooms gill-side-down for about 7 minutes or until lightly charred around the edges. Flip the mushrooms over and place the cheese onto the gill side of the mushroom. Grill the mushrooms another 3 minutes or until the cheese has melted and the mushroom is nicely marked by the grill grates.

Serve each mushroom on a bun and top with a teaspoon of BBQ sauce and about a ¼ cup of BBQ Slaw.

Makes 6 sandwiches.

VEGETARIAN ROASTED RED PEPPER AND OLIVE MUFFULETTA

Every time we go to New Orleans, we have to grab a muffuletta. Many folks argue over who makes the best one, but really, they're all delicious. What's not to love when there's delicious bread, meaty olive dressing, spicy Creole mustard, and melted cheese?

Before you make this classic sandwich, be sure to visit the olive bar at almost any specialty store. It's best to select a mix of different kinds of olives in order to add to the complexity of the dish. Be sure to grab plenty from the spicy bin to give your olive dressing some kick. We also like to use fresh cauliflower and carrots in place of pickled ones. This cuts down on the salt in the dish and makes it more palatable.

Muffuletta bread may be tough to find outside of the South; if it isn't available at your local deli, just use a light focaccia bread in its place.

2 cups spicy, pitted olives (green, black, and kalamata)

1 large rib celery (about ½ cup, sliced)

1 ½ cups thinly sliced cauliflower

1 medium carrot (about ½ cup sliced)

1 ½ teaspoons Italian seasoning mix

3 cloves garlic, crushed

¾ cup olive oil

¾ cup white vinegar

2 10-inch muffuletta breads

2 tablespoons olive oil mayonnaise, divided

4 tablespoons Creole mustard, divided

14 ounces sliced cheese (Provolone or Swiss)

4 roasted red peppers (fresh or jarred)

2 medium tomatoes (sliced)

2 cups chopped romaine lettuce (optional)

12 pepperoncini peppers (on the side)

Using the slicer blade on your food processor, slice the olives, celery, cauliflower, and carrot. Place the sliced vegetables into a 2-quart container; add the Italian seasoning mix, crushed garlic, olive oil, and vinegar. Allow the mixture to marinate and the flavors to meld for a day. The longer you leave it, the better it will be.

Preheat your oven to 350 degrees F. Slice the muffuletta bread in half. On the bottom half of each, spread half of the olive dressing. On the top slices, spread one tablespoon of mayonnaise and two tablespoons of Creole mustard and then add half of the cheese on each in an even layer.

Place the top halves on a baking sheet in the oven for 15 minutes or until the cheese is melted. Pile the roasted red peppers, tomatoes, and lettuce on top of the olive dressing. Place the top on each sandwich. Slice into quarters. Serve immediately with peppers.

Makes 2 large sandwiches, which is enough for 6 to 8 servings.

SIMPLE AND EASY PORCINI MUSHROOM VEGGIE BURGERS

We've experimented with lots of recipes for homemade veggie burgers, and this may even be "the one"! The tempeh and portobellos add just the right amount of texture, while the mustard and Worcestershire sauce bring in an unmistakable depth of flavor.

These burgers are rich and meaty thanks to the addition of a mere tablespoon of dried porcini mushrooms. If you've never tasted porcini, you are missing out on something great. There's really nothing else like it in the plant world. Chefs will often use dried porcini to give already meaty stews and sauces an even heartier flavor, if that tells you anything about this powerful, pungent mycelium.

1 (8-ounce) package of tempeh, crumbled

1 ½ cups portobello mushrooms, very finely diced

1 tablespoon dried porcini, minced

1 cup shredded smoked Provolone cheese

½ cup minced shallots

½ teaspoon iodized sea salt

½ teaspoon garlic powder

1 teaspoon vegetarian Worcestershire sauce

Cracked black pepper (to taste)

1 tablespoon grainy or Creole mustard

1 tablespoon tomato paste

2 eggs, beaten

¼ cup all-purpose flour

¼ cup canola oil (for frying)

4 to 6 ounces Cheddar cheese, sliced

4 soft sesame buns

1 cup chopped romaine lettuce

1 large tomato, sliced

¼ cup sliced shallots

½ cup dill pickle slices

2 tablespoons grainy or Creole mustard

2 tablespoons olive oil mayonnaise

Mix the tempeh, portobello mushrooms, porcini, cheese, shallots, sea salt, garlic powder, Worcestershire sauce, pepper, mustard, tomato paste, eggs, and flour in a large bowl and work it with your hands until all ingredients are thoroughly mixed. Allow the mixture to rest in the fridge for at least 10 minutes before forming the patties.

In a 10-inch frying pan, heat the oil over medium heat. Portion the patties using a ½-cup measuring cup. Form a 3 ½-inch patty with your hands. Press the sides with your thumb so they are smooth and not craggy. This will help keep your burger together. Once you have formed the patty, place it directly into the hot oil. Panfry in the oil for about 4 minutes per side or until it's lightly browned and the egg has set. Remove the patties from the pan and serve immediately, or set them aside on a paper towel–lined plate until you are ready to take the optional step of grilling the burgers.

Once you have all of your toppings ready, preheat your outdoor grill to 500 degrees F. Cook the burger patties for 3 minutes per side—or until they are well-marked by the grill grates and heated through. This step adds a depth to the flavor. Top the burgers with the cheese slices and allow the heat from the burgers to melt it. Serve on a soft sesame bun with romaine lettuce, sliced tomato, thinly sliced shallots, dill pickle slices, mustard, and mayonnaise.

Makes 4 burgers.

VEGAN SLOPPY JOES

These sloppy joes are such a crowd-pleaser. They come together quickly and make a great, easy family-style meal. What a good way to make sure everybody eats their vegetables!

3 tablespoons olive oil, divided

16 to 20 ounces of any combination of mushrooms, diced

1 vegetable bouillon cube

1 white onion, diced (about 1 cup)

¼ cup white wine (like Pinot Grigio)

2 large carrots, diced (about 1 cup)

2 stalks celery, diced (about ½ cup)

1 green bell pepper, diced (about 1 cup)

1 ½ cups prepared lentils

1 cup ketchup

2 teaspoons vegetarian Worcestershire sauce

1 teaspoon mustard

Sea salt flakes and cracked black pepper (to taste)

8 whole wheat buns, warmed

In a 12-inch frying pan warm 2 tablespoons of the olive oil in medium-high heat. Sauté the mushrooms in the oil until they are brown and the liquid has evaporated. Remove from the pan.

Crumble the bouillon cube. In the same pan, add 1 tablespoon of olive oil and sauté the onion and bouillon crumbles until the onion is translucent. The bouillon cube will melt into the onion as you stir. Deglaze the pan with white wine. Cook until the wine has evaporated, about 4 minutes. Add the carrots, celery, and bell pepper. Cook over medium heat for 5 minutes or until the carrots have softened.

Return the mushrooms to the pan with the vegetables; add the lentils, ketchup, Worcestershire sauce, and mustard. Turn the heat to low, and stir to heat the mixture through. Salt and pepper to taste. Spoon a cup of the mixture onto a warmed bun.

Makes 8 sandwiches.

SMOKY GRILLED VEGETABLE QUESADILLAS

Almost everyone appreciates a quesadilla. They're always quick and comforting, and here, the addition of smoke from the grill makes this old favorite taste even better.

1 medium poblano pepper

1 medium sweet onion, halved (skin left on)

2 whole portobello mushroom caps, stems removed

1 medium green bell pepper, halved (seeds removed)

1 tablespoon ancho chili powder

2 tablespoons olive oil

Sea salt flakes and cracked black pepper (to taste)

4 10-inch whole-wheat tortillas

3 cups shredded Oaxaca cheese (or mozzarella)

Hot sauce

½ cup sour cream

Light the outdoor grill and leave it on high to preheat. Place the poblano pepper on the grill. Once one side is burned black, turn it and burn the other side. Once the poblano pepper is completely charred, place it in a paper bag to cool.

In a large bowl toss the onion, mushrooms, and green pepper with the ancho chili powder, olive oil, and salt and pepper until the vegetables are coated. Place the mushrooms gill-side-down on the grill. Place the onion and peppers skin side down on the grill. The green peppers will be done first because they're thin. Remove them from the grill once you get some nice grill marks on them. This should take 5 minutes. Turn the mushrooms over after 4 minutes. Allow the onion's skin to burn black. (You will peel it later.) Move the mushrooms to indirect heat. Allow the mushrooms to cook until tender, which should take 6 minutes. Once all the vegetables have been removed from the grill and are cool enough to handle, you can begin to prepare them for the quesadilla.

Remove the burnt skin and seeds from the poblano. Remove the burnt onion's skin. Discard skins and seeds. Slice all the vegetables into long, thin strips. Portion the vegetables onto half of each tortilla. Cover with shredded cheese and fold the tortilla. Turn the grill down to medium-low. Grill the quesadillas until they are nicely marked by the grill grates and the cheese has melted. Serve with hot sauce and sour cream.

Makes 4 quesadillas.

TRIPLE TOMATO SOUP WITH TOASTED WHITE CHEDDAR CROUTON

This recipe is a grown-up combination with the "dunk" of the grilled cheese into tomato soup built right into the dish. The deep flavor of this soup comes from three tomato sources: the smokiness of roasted Roma tomatoes, the complexity of sun-dried tomatoes, and the sweetness of tomato paste.

5 large Roma tomatoes, peeled*

1 tablespoon olive oil

2 tablespoons unsalted butter, divided

2 cups thinly sliced white onion

2 tablespoons brandy

1 tablespoon vegetarian Worcestershire sauce

½ cup dry packed sun-dried tomatoes (sliced into ¼-inch strips)

2 tablespoons tomato paste

1 cup water

3 cups vegetable broth

1 teaspoon fresh thyme (4 sprigs)

Sea salt flakes and cracked black pepper (to taste)

4 slices whole-grain bread

1 cup shredded white Cheddar cheese

Turn the broiler on high. Slice the peeled tomatoes lengthwise and place them cut side down on a rimmed baking sheet. Brush each tomato with olive oil and place under the broiler until the tomatoes start to blacken. This takes 8 to 10 minutes; keep your eye on them. Once they're done, set the baking sheet aside and allow the tomatoes to cool.

In a Dutch oven or other heavy pot, heat 1 tablespoon of butter over medium-low heat. Once the butter has melted, add the sliced onion. Allow the onion to sweat down and start to brown; this should take 15 minutes. Add the brandy and the Worcestershire sauce to the pot and raise the heat to medium. Allow most of the liquid to evaporate and then add the sun-dried tomatoes, tomato paste, water, and broth. Add the roasted Roma tomatoes and smash them against the side of the pot using the back of a wooden spoon. This produces a texture that matches well with the onion. Bring the soup to a boil, cover, reduce to low heat, and simmer for at least 20 minutes. Add fresh thyme, salt, and pepper just before serving.

To serve, slather toasted bread with melted butter. Turn the broiler on medium. Divide the soup between two oven-safe bowls, float the toast on top of the soup, and cover the toast with the white Cheddar. Place the bowls under the broiler for 2 to 3 minutes or until the cheese is bubbling. Serve immediately.

Makes 4 servings as a first course or 2 as a main dish.

CURRIED CAULIFLOWER SOUP

We always have a delicious cauliflower soup every year at Christmastime. It's unclear how curried cauliflower soup became a part of the family tradition, but somehow it did. Here is our version with red curry paste and basil oil that is sure to make an appearance on your table this holiday season.

1 large head cauliflower, broken into florets, stems chopped (4 to 5 cups)

3 tablespoons canola oil, divided

1 ½ cups diced onion (about 1 medium)

2 tablespoons red curry paste

Zest of 1 lemon (about 1 teaspoon)

½ cup white wine (like Pinot Grigio)

1 ½ cups vegetable stock

1 can light coconut milk

1 tablespoon rice vinegar

½ teaspoon cane sugar

Sea salt flakes and cracked black pepper (to taste)

1 tablespoon basil oil or chopped fresh basil

Thinly sliced hot peppers (optional)

¼ cup chopped green onions or chives (to garnish)

Preheat your oven to 375 degrees F. Toss the cauliflower in 2 tablespoons of canola oil and spread onto a large baking sheet; roast until the tips of the cauliflower are golden brown, about 15 minutes. Remove the cauliflower from the oven.

In a large soup pot over medium heat, sweat the onion in the remaining tablespoon of canola oil until translucent, about 3 minutes. Add the curry paste and lemon zest. Raise the heat to medium-high and add the wine. Cook until most of the wine has evaporated.

Add all of the cauliflower stems and half of the florets to the pot, along with the vegetable stock, coconut milk, vinegar, and sugar. Using an immersion blender, blend the soup until smooth. Check for seasoning and add salt and pepper if needed. Ladle the soup into a bowl, top with ¼ cup of the roasted cauliflower florets, a drizzle of basil oil or fresh basil, hot peppers, and a sprinkling of chives.

Makes 4 servings as a first course or 2 as a main dish.

SAFFRON EGG DROP SOUP

How does one arrive at a Chinese/Spanish fusion soup in the South? I think back happily to the times when, as a child, I would go out to lunch after church every Sunday with my family. Most weeks we'd end up at a place called Nam King on Summer Avenue in East Memphis. My dad would order something like deep-fried chicken feet just to watch us all squirm, but I would always order egg drop soup.

What I picture most is the color of the broth: such a deep yellow it almost seemed like a cartoon drawing of what this particular soup should look like. With this recipe, we recreated that color by including saffron threads in the broth. Since that step led to a Spanish flavor profile, adding Manchego cheese and sherry vinegar sealed the deal. We updated this traditional soup even more by replacing the crunch of the fried noodles with diced vegetables.

½ cup finely diced red bell pepper (about 1 small)

½ cup finely diced purple onion (about 1 small)

½ cup finely diced green tomato (about 1 medium)

2 tablespoons finely chopped flat-leaf parsley

1 tablespoon olive oil

½ teaspoon sherry vinegar

¼ teaspoon cane sugar

Sea salt flakes and cracked black pepper (to taste)

Saffron Broth (recipe follows)

3 eggs, beaten

½ cup shredded Manchego cheese

Add the pepper, onion, and tomato into a small bowl. Add the parsley to the mixture, along with the olive oil, sherry vinegar, and sugar. Add salt and pepper to taste. Set this mixture aside since it's the garnish for the soup.

Bring the Saffron Broth to a rolling boil. Add the beaten eggs to the boiling broth—one small spoonful at a time—until all the beaten eggs are used. (The splintering effect is really cool to watch!) To serve, spoon the egg and broth mixture into a bowl, top with a spoonful of the vegetable mixture, and then sprinkle a bit of the Manchego on top.

Makes 4 servings as a first course or 2 as a main dish.

SAFFRON BROTH

1 quart vegetable stock

½ quart water

5 cloves garlic, minced

Zest of 1 lemon

Zest of 1 orange

¼ teaspoon saffron threads

1 teaspoon sherry vinegar

Sea salt flakes and cracked black pepper (to taste)

Over medium-high heat add the vegetable stock, water, and garlic to the pot. Add the lemon zest, orange zest, saffron, and sherry vinegar. Simmer over medium heat for 20 minutes. Add salt and pepper to taste.

Makes 1 quart.

WATERMELON AND TOMATO GAZPACHO

Summer watermelon and summer tomatoes, married at last. The first time we tried this so-strange-but-so-good combination, we swooned. When tomatoes were at their peak in July, this dish was the first thing out to the tables at our five-course all-tomato dinner. We've served it countless times since then.

- 1 medium jalapeño (seeds removed if you like it mild)
- 2 cups roughly chopped tomatoes
- 1 ½ cups roughly chopped green bell pepper (about 2 medium)
- ¼ cup loose-packed fresh cilantro
- Juice of 1 lime (about 1 tablespoon)
- 1 large clove garlic, minced
- 1 tablespoon sherry vinegar
- ¼ teaspoon sea salt flakes
- ¼ teaspoon cracked black pepper
- ½ teaspoon ancho chili powder
- 1 cup watermelon juice (Use a juicer or blend and strain 2 to 3 cups of watermelon flesh.)
- 1 avocado, sliced (to garnish)
- 2 cups croutons (to garnish)
- ¼ cup sliced green onion (to garnish)
- 2 hard-boiled eggs, chopped (to garnish)

Place the following ingredients into the work bowl of your food processor: the jalapeño, tomatoes, bell peppers, cilantro, lime juice, garlic, vinegar, salt, pepper, and ancho chili powder. Pulse the food processor four times for less than 2 seconds at a time until the ingredients are finely chopped but still distinct and recognizable; don't blend it too smooth. Add the vegetable mixture to the watermelon juice and chill for 20 minutes to allow the flavors to come together.

Ladle the soup into a bowl and pile on the garnishes: avocado, croutons, green onion, and eggs.

Makes 4 servings as a first course or 2 as a main dish.

MEXICAN CORN CHOWDER

One of our favorite things in the world is a dish known as elote con mayonesa. It's Mexican street food at its best: boiled corn brushed with mayo and then sprinkled with Cotija cheese, chili salt, and a squeeze of lime. This chowder has the same wonderful flavor combination.

7 medium ears of corn (about 4 cups of kernels; frozen is fine)

1 ½ cups diced onion (about 1 medium)

1 tablespoon olive oil

4 cups vegetable broth

1 tablespoon minced chipotle pepper (from a can)

3 cloves garlic, smashed

1 teaspoon ancho chili powder

1 teaspoon iodized sea salt

½ cup crumbled Cotija cheese (use feta cheese if Cotija is unavailable)

1 cup loose-packed cilantro leaves

½ cup sour cream (optional)

1 lime, sliced into wedges

Peel the corn and remove all the silks by running a wet paper towel over the kernels. Remove the kernels by standing the ear on its end and carefully running a sharp knife down the length of the ear of corn on all sides. Do this in a large bowl. In a large soup pot over medium-high heat, sweat the onion in a tablespoon of olive oil. Once the onion starts to brown, add the broth, chipotle pepper, garlic, and 3 cups of the corn kernels. Bring the soup to a boil by raising the heat to high. Then reduce to a simmer, cover, and allow the mixture to cook for 10 minutes. Remove from the heat and blend the mixture smooth with an immersion blender. Return the soup to the stovetop and add the remaining 1 cup of corn for texture.

Mix the ancho chili powder and the sea salt together in a small bowl to make chili salt. Ladle the chowder into a bowl, and top with a ¼ teaspoon of chili salt, a tablespoon of Cotija cheese, a few cilantro leaves, a spoonful of sour cream, and a squeeze of lime.

Makes 4 servings as a first course or 2 as a main dish.

THE CHUBBY VEGETARIAN GUMBO

Many times vegetarian gumbo is just the same old meaty gumbo with the meat left out of the mix. The problem with that approach is that much of the flavor—smoke, salt, and savoriness—is derived from those meat sources. Here we've used a method traditionally used in Indian cookery to make rich curries and infused some of those flavors back in by using soy sauce and liquid smoke. The idea is to make a paste from garlic, onions, vegetables, and spices to flavor the whole dish so that everything else in the pot will be perfectly delicious.

2 tablespoons canola oil

2 tablespoons all-purpose flour

1 cup chopped tomato (1 medium)

1 ½ cups chopped onion (1 medium)

8 cloves garlic

1 tablespoon vegetarian Worcestershire sauce

2 tablespoon Creole mustard

1 ½ teaspoons liquid smoke

1 tablespoon vinegar

½ teaspoon hot sauce

1 teaspoon soy sauce

1 teaspoon dried thyme

1 teaspoon red pepper flakes

1 tablespoon smoked paprika

¼ teaspoon nutmeg

1 teaspoon dried oregano

1 quart vegetable stock

4 cups sliced okra (¼-inch slices, stem-end discarded)

1 ½ cups red beans (1 16-ounce can, drained and rinsed, or make your own)

10 ounces crimini mushrooms, quartered

1 ½ cups diced zucchini (1 medium)

1 ½ cups diced green pepper (1 large)

1 ½ cups diced red pepper (1 large)

1 cup thinly sliced celery (2 ribs)

4 to 5 cups cooked jasmine rice

½ cup sliced green onion (to garnish)

5 to 6 sprigs baby dill (to garnish)

To make the roux, place the canola oil and flour into a cold medium-size Dutch oven. This is the pot in which you will eventually make the gumbo. A heavy pot like this is essential when making a roux because of its ability to distribute heat evenly. With the oil and flour in the Dutch oven, turn the heat on medium. Whisk the mixture constantly until you notice that it has become nutty and fragrant, both of which happen about 5 minutes into the process. (It will smell a bit like fried chicken.) At this point, turn the heat to low. Keep a close eye on your roux, and whisk the mixture about every minute so that no part of the roux burns. Continue in this fashion for another 20 minutes or until the roux has taken on the color of an old penny. Remove the pot from the heat.

Into the work bowl of your food processor, place the tomato, onion, garlic, Worcestershire sauce, mustard, liquid smoke, vinegar, hot sauce, soy sauce, thyme, red pepper flakes, paprika, nutmeg, and oregano. (This may be an unconventional method for making gumbo, but it works beautifully.) Blend the mixture until smooth. This is your flavoring agent for the whole dish.

continued next page ▶

Now return the Dutch oven with the roux still in it to a burner set to medium-high heat, and immediately add to it the mixture you just made in the food processor. Stir to incorporate. Continue cooking and stirring the resulting mixture until most of the liquid has evaporated and it resembles a paste. Add the vegetable stock and stir. Once the mixture is heated through, turn the burner to medium-low. Add the okra, red beans, mushrooms, zucchini, green and red peppers, and celery to the pot. Cook uncovered for 20 minutes until everything is heated through, but not mush.

To serve, ladle gumbo into a bowl and top with about ½ cup of rice, a few green onions, and a sprig of fresh dill. Have plenty of crusty French bread and butter on hand for sopping up the amazing broth.

Makes 8 servings.

TIP: If you like okra but are not a fan of the sliminess that can sometimes occur with it, heat 1 tablespoon of canola oil in a frying pan and then sauté the sliced okra in batches until lightly browned. Add the cooked okra to the gumbo. Problem solved!

VEGETARIAN FROGMORE STEW

Traditionally, Frogmore Stew is served with cocktail sauce, garlic butter, and rolls. This really is a dish meant to feed a crowd. When it's ready, all the goodies are picked up out of the flavorful broth and dumped onto a table covered with newspaper. Once it's cool enough to touch, you just grab what you like and start dipping the corn into the butter or the potatoes into the cocktail sauce. It's all very lively and festive.

So what's in a vegetarian version of this mythical dish? We chose to throw in some fresh artichoke hearts and stems, which are fun to eat, and some vegetarian sausage, which works well for this application.

- 1 quart vegetable stock
- 1 quart water
- 12 ounces beer
- 1 lemon
- 1 ½ tablespoons Old Bay (more to garnish)
- ½ teaspoon crushed red pepper flakes
- 10 cloves garlic, smashed, divided
- ½ teaspoon liquid smoke
- ¼ teaspoon cracked black pepper
- 1 teaspoon cane sugar
- Iodized sea salt (to taste)
- 4 cups red-skin new potatoes, cut in half
- 4 ears yellow corn, shucked and cut into quarters
- 1 pound vegetarian sausage (such as our Vegetarian Boudin on page 151,) cut into quarters
- 4 fresh artichokes, trimmed*
- 2 tablespoons unsalted butter
- ¼ cup cocktail sauce
- ¼ cup chopped fresh parsley

In a large stock pot over high heat, pour in the stock, water, and beer. Next, cut the lemon in half, squeeze the juice into the pot, and then drop the squeezed lemon into the pot as well. Add the Old Bay seasoning, crushed red pepper flakes, 8 cloves of garlic, liquid smoke, black pepper, and sugar. Check for seasoning and adjust the salt to your taste—it may not need any depending on how salty the vegetable stock was to start. Bring the whole mixture up to a boil. Carefully add the potatoes and cook for about 8 minutes. Add the corn, sausage, and artichokes to the mixture. Cook uncovered for another 10 minutes or until the potatoes are tender. Fish a variety of the components out of the broth and into a bowl. Add just ½ cup of the broth for the steam and aroma.

While the stew cools a bit, place butter in a microwave-safe dish, along with the 2 reserved garlic cloves. Microwave for 30 seconds until the butter is just melted. Serve your Vegetarian Frogmore Stew garnished with a light sprinkling of Old Bay and a pinch of fresh parsley with garlic butter and cocktail sauce on the side. No need for a fork—just use your hands.

Makes 4 servings.

*For the artichokes: Cut off and discard the top ⅔ of the bulb, leaving the whole stem and the bottom ⅓ of the bulb intact. (There is very little meat in the top portion of the vegetable.) Using a spoon, scoop out the choke, the fibrous center part of the vegetable. Using a vegetable peeler, peel the stem to reveal the tender and edible inside part of the stem. Finally, cut ½ inch off the tip of the stem, stand the artichoke up on the bulb-side, and cut into quarters by running your knife through the stem, heart, and remaining leaves. This leaves you with a few leaves to pull off and scrape out when you are eating the stew, but most importantly, it leaves the heart and stem, the most delicious parts.

NOTE: *We recommend using fresh artichoke hearts, but frozen ones will do in a pinch.*

MAIN COURSES

Vegetarian Country Captain 119

Vegetarian "Chicken" and Waffles 122

Tacos with Spicy, Smoky Lentils 125

20-Minute Tamales 126

Stuffed Portobello Mushroom Wellington 128

Peach and Tarragon Pesto Pizza 131

Zucchini and Tomato Galette 133

Vegetarian "Chicken" Pot Pie 134

Chanterelle and Apricot Stuffed Acorn Squash with Miracle Mushroom Gravy 136

Chicken-Fried Portobello with Mushroom and Shallot Gravy 138

BBQ Tofu Pizza 140

Artichoke Hearts and Succotash over Smoked Cheddar Grits 143

Vegetarian "Chicken" with Parsley and Olive Oil Dumplings 146

Dirty Fried Rice, King Oyster Mushroom "Scallops," and Creole Coconut Sauce 147

Vegetarian Boudin Sausage 151

Smoked Cheddar Jalapeño Cornbread 153

Vegetarian Meatballs 154

Tofu Almondine in a White Wine-Butter Sauce 157

Ratatouille Napoleon 159

Vegan Peanut Chili with Charred Corn and Avocado Salsa 162

Porcini and Portobello Mushroom Bourguignon over Smashed Potatoes 163

Vegetarian Meatloaf with Garlic Mashed Potatoes 166

Vegetarian Red Beans and Rice with Andouille Eggplant 170

Memphis-Style Dry Rub BBQ Tofu 173

Butternut Squash Rotini Mac and Cheese 175

VEGETARIAN COUNTRY CAPTAIN

How did curry, with its roots in Asia, make its way into so many of our grandmothers' recipes, and why is this exotic spice found in community cookbooks all over the South? In our family, we have had curried cauliflower soup at Christmas for as long as I can remember. But why?

One day we heard the story behind a Carolina dish called Country Captain, which had its heyday in the 1950s country club scene. Legend has it that a British sea captain who was working in the spice trade introduced the dish and the spices required to make it to Southern port cities like Charleston and Savannah. From there, adventuresome Southerners made it their own.

Our County Captain is made with thick, hearty slices of eggplant rather than chicken. The spongy eggplant soaks up all the wonderful spices. This is the perfect thing to make for a crowd—it'll easily feed six people, and because it's a casserole, it requires very little hands-on time.

1 medium onion, peeled and roughly chopped

1 medium tomato, roughly chopped

3-inch piece fresh ginger, peeled, roughly chopped

10 cloves garlic

1 medium jalapeño, stem removed

1 apple, peeled and cut away from the core

1 cup loose-packed cilantro (more to garnish)

Zest of 1 lime

1 tablespoon white vinegar

2 tablespoons unsalted butter (use soy or olive oil margarine to make this vegan)

1 teaspoon coriander

1 teaspoon cumin

¼ teaspoon turmeric

2 teaspoons hot curry powder

1 teaspoon iodized sea salt

1 teaspoon cane sugar

1 (13.5-ounce) can coconut milk

1 cup vegetable broth

1 tablespoon sambal (optional)

1 2-inch cinnamon stick

¼ cup golden raisins

2 cups peeled, diced potatoes (about 1 large)

1 ½ cups prepared garbanzo beans (or 1 can, drained)

1 ½ cups diced green pepper (about 1 large)

2 medium Italian eggplants

Sea salt flakes and cracked black pepper (to taste)

3 cups prepared jasmine rice

1 cup toasted sliced almonds (to garnish)

Fresh cilantro (to garnish)

Lime wedges (to garnish)

Into the work bowl of your food processor add the onion, tomato, ginger, garlic, jalapeño, apple, cilantro, lime zest, and vinegar. Blend for 3 minutes or until smooth.

Preheat your oven to 350 degrees F. In a Dutch oven over medium-high heat, melt the butter and add the coriander, cumin, turmeric, and curry powder. Stir to incorporate the spices into the butter. Allow them to cook for about a minute or until they become fragrant. Add the mixture from the food processor and stir. Cook until most of the liquid has evaporated, stirring occasionally, until it becomes a thick paste, about 10 minutes.

continued next page ▸

Add the salt, sugar, coconut milk, broth, sambal (if you like it spicy), cinnamon, raisins, potatoes, beans, and green pepper to the pot. Stir, put the lid in place, and reduce the heat to low. Allow the mixture to simmer for 5 minutes while you prepare the eggplant.

Trim the stem end of the eggplant and slice into generous ½-inch slices. You should end up with six good-looking slices and the trimmings from the end. Sprinkle both sides of the pieces with salt and pepper to taste. In a 13 x 9-inch casserole dish, lay the eggplant slices down in a shingle-like pattern. Using a large ladle, spoon the warm mixture from the Dutch oven over the top of the eggplant slices. Cover the dish with foil and place it in the oven for 1 hour.

Using a spatula place 1 large slice of eggplant in the center of a dinner plate. Spoon some of the mixture from the casserole over the top of it. Serve the dish with ¼ cup jasmine rice and garnish with almonds, cilantro leaves, and lime wedges. Add salt and pepper to taste.

Makes 6 servings.

NOTE: *There are a million variations of curry powder. Hot curry powder is a good, basic blend of turmeric, cumin, coriander, ginger, cinnamon, clove, fenugreek, cardamom, fennel seed, and some form of hot chili.*

VEGETARIAN "CHICKEN" AND WAFFLES

This idea was born out of the truffled Scotch egg we concocted with Chef Andrew Adams and served at an event celebrating farmers at the Brooks Museum in Memphis. With culinary awesomeness, Adams showed us how to deep-fry an egg without overcooking the center. His sous vide method yielded a perfect egg: crispy on the outside with a slightly set yolk. It was the hit of the evening.

At home, we don't happen to have an immersion circulator or an industrial fryer (or an incredible kitchen staff full of talented chefs, for that matter), so we figured out how to poach the egg with the flour mixture already in place.

This crispy egg is spiked with the kinds of seasoning you'd normally find in fried chicken. Adding a little truffle salt makes this a really special version of a soul food classic.

Special equipment: four 12 x 12-inch squares microwave-safe plastic wrap, four 4-inch pieces of kitchen twine

¼ teaspoon black truffle salt
½ teaspoon dried sage
½ teaspoon dried thyme

¼ teaspoon garlic powder
¼ teaspoon cracked black pepper
¼ cup all-purpose flour
½ cup panko bread crumbs
4 large eggs
Canola oil (for frying)

4 Belgian waffles (freshly made or frozen)
2 tablespoons chopped fresh parsley (to garnish)
Sea salt flakes and cracked black pepper (to taste)
½ cup warm maple syrup

In a saucepan over medium heat, bring a pot of water at least 3 ½ inches deep to a simmer. In a small bowl, mix together the truffle salt, sage, thyme, garlic powder, pepper, flour, and panko bread crumbs.

Lay the four sheets of plastic wrap flat on your work surface. Scatter 2 tablespoons of the spiced flour in a single layer over the center 5 inches of each plastic wrap sheet. Crack 1 egg on the center of each. Gather the corners of the plastic wrap. Place the corners into one hand. With the other hand, grab the egg bundle and twist while being sure to push out any air. Tie the twisted portion with the string. Repeat for each.

Prepare an ice bath in a medium bowl. Place the egg bundles into the simmering water for 5 to 7 minutes. At 5 minutes, the white will be set, but the yolk will still be runny. If you like your yolk more set, leave the bundle in the water for 7 minutes. When the eggs are done, remove the bundles and place them into an ice bath while they're still wrapped in plastic.

In a small saucepan over medium-high heat, bring the canola oil up to 350 degrees F. The oil should be at least 2 ½ inches deep in the pan. Using kitchen shears, snip the plastic just below where it was tied. Carefully unwrap the egg. Using a slotted spoon, lower the egg into the oil for a total of 1 minute or until it's golden brown.

To serve, place one egg atop a warm waffle. Garnish with parsley, salt, and pepper, plus a drizzle of maple syrup.

Makes 4 servings.

TIP: If you're serving this to friends or at a dinner party, you can do all the steps up to the frying beforehand. Then when your guests are hungry, dinner will come together quickly.

TACOS WITH SPICY, SMOKY LENTILS

Warm weather means it's time for hot and spicy Mexican food. Give us some migas, chilaquiles, guacamole, tortas, stuffed chilies, whatever, as long as it's spicy.

This is one of the simplest and tastiest vegetarian "meat" recipes out there due to a double infusion of smoke from the chipotle powder and the smoked sun-dried tomatoes. It's also versatile. Use this filling in a taco, or try it in a burrito or as stuffing for tamales (page 126). The texture of the lentils matches what most of us think of when we think of taco meat.

2 tablespoons olive oil

1 cup diced white onion (about 1 small)

1 teaspoon cumin

½ teaspoon sea salt flakes

½ teaspoon ancho chili powder

½ teaspoon chipotle chili powder

1 tablespoon tomato paste

½ teaspoon toasted sesame oil

1 cup dry brown lentils

1 ½ cups water

1 tablespoon white vinegar

¼ cup smoked sun-dried tomatoes, finely chopped

Simple Smoky Salsa (page 223)

12 small corn or flour tortillas or taco shells, warmed

1 cup shredded smoked Cheddar cheese

2 cups finely shredded green cabbage

½ cup chopped green onion

2 avocados, peeled and sliced

¼ cup sour cream

Lime wedges

Hot sauce

In a saucepan over medium heat, add the olive oil and then sauté the onion. Once the onion is translucent, add the cumin, salt, and chili powders. Allow to cook for about another minute. Add the tomato paste, sesame oil, lentils, water, vinegar, and sun-dried tomatoes, and bring it all up to a boil. Reduce the mixture to a simmer, cover, and allow to cook for 30 minutes or until all the liquid has been absorbed. The lentils should be tender, but not falling apart.

This is best served family-style with the Spicy, Smoky Lentils, Simple Smoky Salsa, tortillas, Cheddar, cabbage, green onion, avocados, sour cream, limes, and hot sauce all set out on the table. That way, each person can make a taco to his or her own specifications.

Makes 4 servings.

20-MINUTE TAMALES

We love tamales, but they can be time-consuming to make. Even just steaming them takes at least an hour. So why not cook the masa, the corn grits used to make tamales, on the stovetop and then roll it in the corn husks with the filling? Using this method knocks a good hour off the time it takes to make this dish!

4 cups vegetable broth

2 tablespoons olive oil

Zest of 1 lime

1 teaspoon ancho chili powder

½ teaspoon baking powder

1 ¼ cups masa (for tamales)

18 corn husks (soaked in water for 1 hour until soft—or simply use parchment)

2 ½ cups Tamale Filling (recipe follows)

Hot sauce (to garnish)

Simple Smoky Salsa (page 223) to garnish

Bring the broth to a boil and add the oil, lime zest, ancho, and baking powder. Stir and then add the masa a little at a time so you don't get any lumps. Cook for 20 minutes, stirring often to develop a creamy texture. While the masa is hot, spread about ¼ cup in the center of a corn husk (or piece of parchment), place two spoonfuls of filling in the center of the masa, and roll it up. You don't need to fold the ends up because the thick masa stays in place. Allow them to cool.

To serve, simply heat the tamales in the microwave for 2 minutes and then top with hot sauce, salsa, and anything else you'd like.

Makes 8 servings.

NOTE: *This recipe freezes well.*

TAMALE FILLING

2 ½ cups Mushroom Meat (page 230)

1 teaspoon cumin

½ teaspoon ancho chili powder

½ teaspoon chipotle powder

Mix the Mushroom Meat, cumin, ancho, and chipotle together in a small bowl and set aside until ready to use.

Makes 2 ½ cups.

STUFFED PORTOBELLO MUSHROOM WELLINGTON

This mushroom main dish is incredible. The meatiness of the grilled mushroom is perfectly complemented by the richness of the stuffing. The puff pastry adds a crunchy texture to the dish, so it all comes together nicely. Think of it as an updated version of an '80s throwback dinner dish that's easy enough for a weeknight, but fancy enough to serve to guests.

½ cup olive oil, divided

¼ cup champagne vinegar

1 teaspoon red miso (or soy sauce, but then omit the salt)

¼ teaspoon sea salt flakes

¼ teaspoon cracked black pepper

4 medium portobello mushrooms

Mushroom Stuffing (recipe follows)

8 sheets phyllo dough

⅛ cup chopped parsley (to garnish)

Whisk ¼ cup of the olive oil, vinegar, miso, salt, and pepper together until well incorporated. Pour the mixture over the gill side of four medium whole portobello mushroom caps. Marinate the mushrooms for 30 minutes. Starting gill-side-down, grill the mushrooms over a high flame for about 4 minutes per side. While the mushrooms are cooking, place a brick or cast-iron skillet on top of them to flatten. Remove and set aside to cool.

Preheat your oven to 375 degrees F. Divide the stuffing among the mushrooms, creating a layer of stuffing on each flat mushroom, and place them on a parchment-lined baking sheet. Using a coffee can as a template and the tip of a sharp knife, cut the puff pastry into rounds that equal the size of the mushroom (about 4 inches across). Brush each round generously with the remaining olive oil, and place rounds on the baking sheet next to the mushrooms. When the pastry is brown, the filling should be cooked through. This should take about 20 minutes.

To serve, top each stuffed mushroom with a puff pastry round and garnish with parsley.

MUSHROOM STUFFING

1 to 1 ½ cups leeks (about 1 large)

1 tablespoon unsalted butter

½ cup apple juice

1 cup button mushrooms, thinly sliced

½ teaspoon fresh thyme leaves (about 3 sprigs)

2 ounces soft goat cheese, crumbled

1 large egg, beaten

¼ cup panko bread crumbs

Sea salt flakes and cracked black pepper (to taste)

Pull the first tough layer off the leek and discard. Starting at the root end, cut ½-inch slices from the leek. Slice the leek until it becomes darker green and tough near the middle. Discard the top and the root end. Using your thumb, push the rings of the leek apart, dropping the individual rings into a large bowl of clean water. Swish the leek rings around in the water to dislodge any dirt. Drain the rings.

In a 10-inch skillet over medium heat, melt the butter and then slowly cook the leeks in the butter. This should take about 15 minutes. Once the leeks have softened, turn up the heat and add the apple juice to deglaze the pan. Cook until most of the liquid has evaporated. Place the leeks in a bowl to cool.

Add the mushrooms to the hot pan and sauté until brown. Next, add the mushrooms to the leek mixture and allow to cool. Add the thyme, goat cheese, egg, and panko, and mix to incorporate. Add salt and pepper to taste. The mixture should come together and be thick, not loose. Add more panko if needed. Set the mixture in the fridge until ready to use.

Makes 4 servings.

PEACH AND TARRAGON PESTO PIZZA

We grill peaches, make ice cream with them, put them into cobblers, and eat them straight off of the tree all summer long. This surprising combination turned out to be our favorite peach dish of the entire season.

1 Beer Pizza Crust (page 224)

½ cup Tarragon Pesto (recipe follows)

5 ripe peaches*, peeled, pitted, and sliced into half-moons (about 2 cups)

3 ounces soft goat cheese, crumbled

Sea salt flakes and cracked black pepper (to taste)

½ cup grated Manchego cheese (to garnish)

Preheat your oven (with the pizza stone in place) to 550 degrees F. Stretch, toss, or roll out your dough to a 10-inch circle. Place a 12-inch piece of parchment on your pizza peel or the back of a parchment-lined baking sheet, place the dough round on the pizza peel, and slide it into the oven. Cook for 2 minutes.

Pull the dough out of the oven and top it first with ½ cup of the pesto, and then the peach slices, and finally, the soft goat cheese. Slide the pizza back onto the stone for another 5 to 7 minutes or until the peaches start to caramelize. Remove and sprinkle with salt, pepper, and grated Manchego cheese.

Makes 4 servings.

*Peel the peaches using a serrated peeler. Frozen peaches can be substituted in this recipe if peaches are not in season.

TARRAGON PESTO

This recipe will make more than you need, so feel free to cut it in half or just make the whole amount. It's great on sandwiches, thinned out and used as a salad dressing, or as a dip for crunchy vegetables.

1 cup zucchini, chopped

4 cloves garlic

¼ cup walnuts

½ cup loose-packed fresh tarragon (leaves from about 5 stems)

Zest of 1 lemon

½ teaspoon cracked black pepper

¼ teaspoon sea salt flakes

¼ cup olive oil

Place the zucchini, garlic, walnuts, tarragon, lemon zest, black pepper, and salt into the food processor, and blend until the mixture has a smooth texture. Drizzle the olive oil into the food processor while it's running in order to emulsify the pesto.

Makes 1 cup.

ZUCCHINI AND TOMATO GALETTE

This simple dish has an elegant presentation. For that reason, it's a great dish to take to a party—a savory galette is sure to get a few oohs and ahhs. Best of all, you can use just about any vegetables you have on hand to make variations of it.

Basic Piecrust Dough
  (page 227)

1 12-inch zucchini, sliced into
  ⅛-inch-thick rounds

4 medium Roma tomatoes
  sliced into ⅛-inch-
  thick rounds

2 large eggs, beaten

½ cup whole-milk
  ricotta cheese

2 cloves garlic, minced

1 teaspoon champagne
  vinegar

½ teaspoon minced
  fresh oregano

Sea salt flakes and cracked
  black pepper (to taste)

¼ cup shredded Parmesan
  cheese (to garnish)

Roll the piecrust into a 16 x 11-inch rectangle and place it on a parchment-lined 17 x 12-inch baking sheet. Leaving a ½-inch margin of crust around the outside, arrange the zucchini and tomatoes in a shingle-like pattern on the crust. Fold extra crust up over the edge of the vegetables and pinch the corners to seal them together.

In a bowl whisk the eggs, ricotta, garlic, vinegar, oregano, salt, and pepper together until well incorporated. Slowly pour the mixture evenly over the vegetables. Bake at 350 degrees F. for 50 minutes. Garnish with Parmesan cheese. Serve at room temperature or warm.

Makes 4 servings.

VEGETARIAN "CHICKEN" POT PIE

Faux chicken pot pie is one of the all-time most popular posts at The Chubby Vegetarian blog. This tasty version is what we often make for a vegetarian main dish at Thanksgiving. Feel free to substitute diced-up some mushrooms or your favorite meat substitute in the place of the seitan if you please.

1 pound "Chicken-Style" seitan, diced

¼ cup plus 1 tablespoon all-purpose flour, divided

2 tablespoons canola oil

1 cup diced carrots (about 2 medium)

1 cup diced green bell pepper (about 1 large)

1 ½ cup peeled, diced Idaho potato

1 ½ cups green peas (frozen)

¼ cup minced fresh flat-leaf parsley

½ cup diced shallots

½ cup diced celery (about two ribs)

½ teaspoon sea salt flakes

½ teaspoon dried thyme

½ teaspoon garlic powder

1 ½ teaspoons champagne vinegar

1 ½ tablespoons unsalted butter

1 cup 2% milk

1 cup vegetable stock

Basic Piecrust (page 227)

Sea salt flakes and cracked black pepper (to taste)

1 egg

2 tablespoons of water

Toss diced seitan and ¼ cup flour together in a medium-size bowl. In a large Dutch oven over medium-high heat, add the canola oil. Once the oil starts to shimmer, add the seitan mixture. Allow it to cook undisturbed for 4 minutes until golden brown. Stir the pot and cook for another 2 minutes. Remove the crispy seitan from the pot and set it aside on a paper towel to drain. Add the carrots, pepper, potato, peas, parsley, shallots, celery, salt, thyme, garlic powder, and vinegar to the pot and stir.

After the vegetables have been cooking for 4 minutes, push them up against the wall of the pot to form a well in the center. Add 1 tablespoon flour and the butter to the well and whisk until they form a paste. Cook the paste, also known as a roux, another 2 minutes until fragrant and lightly browned. Add the milk, stock, and reserved seitan to the pot. Stir, bring to a quick boil by raising the temperature to medium-high, and then remove from the heat.

Preheat your oven to 400 degrees F. Cut the rested dough ball in half. Roll one half out to about 11 or 12 inches, and place it in the bottom of a 10-inch pie pan. Cook the crust in the oven for 8 to 10 minutes or until lightly browned. The crust may puff, but it will still be supple enough to pour the filling on top. Pour in the prepared filling. Roll the second half of the dough out to about 11 inches for the lid. Place the lid on the pie. Using kitchen shears cut off the excess and crimp the edges with your finger to seal the top and bottom crusts together. With the shears cut eight vents in the top of the pie. Place the pie on a baking sheet in case it overflows in the oven. Cook 20 minutes.

To make an egg wash, beat the egg and water together in a small bowl. Brush the top crust with the egg wash, sprinkle on some sea salt, and bake another 10 minutes until the crust is golden brown.

Makes 4 servings.

CHANTERELLE AND APRICOT STUFFED ACORN SQUASH WITH MIRACLE MUSHROOM GRAVY

Every year, we try to come up with a vegetarian dish that'll steal the poor turkey's thunder at Thanksgiving. This year, we decided on acorn squash paired with two favorite mushrooms: chanterelle and porcini. The addition of the dried apricots to the stuffing amplifies the earthy, sweet flavor of the chanterelles. Slicing the squash shows off its scalloped edges and makes for a particularly beautiful presentation. The unusual addition of barley to the gravy adds body and texture, and the fried sage sends this dish over the top.

This recipe yields one stuffed acorn squash, which will feed two to three, so adjust the number of squash according to how many guests you are expecting. Make extra—even the omnivores will love this one. You can make it a day ahead of time and store it in the fridge until you're ready to bake it.

1 tablespoon unsalted butter

½ cup finely diced celery

1 cup finely diced white onion (about 1 small)

1 vegetable bouillon cube

¼ cup white wine (like Pinot Grigio)

1 cup chanterelles, torn into strips

¼ cup finely diced dried apricots

Sea salt flakes and cracked black pepper (to taste)

2 cups brioche or good-quality white bread, torn into pieces

2 large eggs, beaten

1 large acorn squash (or 2 small)

2 tablespoons olive oil

Miracle Mushroom Gravy page 8 to garnish

Preheat your oven to 375 degrees. In a medium pan over medium heat, melt the butter and then sauté the celery, onion, and bouillon cube until lightly browned. Deglaze the pan with the wine, and reduce until most of the liquid has evaporated. Add the chanterelles and apricots to the pan and warm through. Add salt and pepper. Chill the mushroom mixture thoroughly. In a large bowl mix the bread, eggs, and the cooled vegetable mixture.

Using a sharp kitchen knife (and plenty of caution), trim the stem end off of the squash and cut the squash into ¾ inch rings. (You should be able to get 4 rings out of a large acorn squash.) Discard the stem end and bottom piece. Using a spoon, scrape the seeds and membrane out of the squash and discard. Lay the squash rings out on a large parchment-lined baking sheet. Drizzle rings with olive oil and bake for 15 minutes.

Remove squash from the oven and press the stuffing into the center of each squash ring. Bake for an additional 15 to 20 minutes or until the stuffing has set and starting to brown. Add Miracle Mushroom Gravy to garnish.

Makes 2 servings.

CHICKEN-FRIED PORTOBELLO WITH MUSHROOM AND SHALLOT GRAVY

I used to eat chicken-fried steak all the time when I was a kid. My grandmother would make it, and we'd have the same conversation every time. "What is it, Mamaw?" I'd ask, "Chicken or steak?" She would joke around and tell me it was both. Though her food was always delicious, I like this meatless version best. A meaty portobello mushroom stands in for steak in our vegetarian take on a Southern classic.

- 1 cup all-purpose flour
- 1 teaspoon sea salt flakes
- 1 teaspoon garlic powder
- 1 teaspoon cracked black pepper
- 1 teaspoon sweet paprika
- 2 large eggs, beaten
- 2 tablespoons heavy cream
- 3 medium portobello mushrooms
- 1 cup canola oil
- Mushroom and Shallot Gravy (recipe follows)
- ¼ cup finely chopped fresh parsley

Combine the flour with the salt, garlic powder, pepper, and paprika in a bowl large enough to accommodate one mushroom at a time. In a separate bowl combine the eggs and cream.

Trim the mushrooms by removing the stems and the part of the cap that hangs over the gill side. (Doing this will create a flat surface, which will make it much easier to panfry the mushrooms.) Reserve the trimmings because you will use them in the gravy.

Heat the oil to medium-high in a 12-inch frying pan. Depending on the size of the mushrooms, this pan should accommodate all three at once. Preheat your oven to 350 degrees F. Now, batter the mushrooms using a three-step process: toss them in the flour mixture, coat them with the egg mixture, and then coat again in the flour mixture. This should help plenty of spiced flour to adhere to the mushroom. Fry the mushrooms for 2 minutes per side or until golden brown.

Place the mushrooms on a baking sheet and finish cooking them through in the oven. This should take 15 minutes, which is the perfect amount of time to make the gravy. To serve, smother each mushroom with the Mushroom and Shallot Gravy and garnish with chopped parsley.

Makes 2 servings.

MUSHROOM AND SHALLOT GRAVY

- 1 tablespoon unsalted butter
- Trimmings from the mushrooms, finely chopped
- ½ cup shallots, minced
- 1 tablespoon all-purpose flour
- ¾ cup broth (preferably mushroom)
- ½ cup 2% milk
- Sea salt flakes (to taste)
- ½ teaspoon cracked black pepper

Melt the butter in a 10-inch frying pan over medium heat. Add the trimmings and shallots. Once the shallots are translucent, add the flour and cook until nutty and fragrant. Add the broth and milk as you whisk. Slowly bring the mixture to a boil and then reduce the heat to low. The gravy should be thick like pancake batter after a few minutes. Season with salt and pepper.

Makes 2 cups.

BBQ TOFU PIZZA

This is one of our favorite dishes here at The Chubby Vegetarian. This pie gets a double hit of smoke from the mozzarella and the BBQ sauce, both of which make it super-savory and awesome. As a bonus, the beer in the crust adds even more flavor.

We make pizza for guests all the time because, well, who doesn't like pizza? Folks are doubtful when they learn that one of the pizzas on the table is BBQ tofu with cabbage. But once they taste this deliciously weird mash-up of Italian and Southern cuisines, they understand why it's one of our favorites.

You can take two shortcuts here if you don't want to make everything from scratch. Use two store-bought pizza crusts—or better yet, some premade pizza dough—and a bottle of your favorite smoky BBQ sauce.

1 block extra-firm tofu

3 tablespoons canola oil

1 cup Chipotle BBQ Sauce (page 226)

Beer Pizza Crust (page 224)

1 cup Vegetable-Packed Tomato Sauce (page 229)

3 cups shredded smoked mozzarella (about 6 ounces, divided)

2 cups shredded purple cabbage, divided

With a pizza stone in place, preheat your oven to 550 degrees F. for at least 40 minutes. This will allow the pizza stone to heat up and crisp the bottom of the pizza.

To prepare our simple BBQ Tofu, cut the tofu into ½-inch cubes. Arrange the cubes on a clean dish towel to allow the excess moisture to drain off the surface of the tofu since this will prevent it from sticking to the pan. Heat a 12-inch frying pan over high heat. Once the pan is hot, add the canola oil. When the oil begins to shimmer, carefully add the dried cubes of tofu to the pan. (If you follow this set of instructions, you shouldn't have a problem with the tofu sticking to the pan. It's all about dry tofu and a very hot pan.) Cook the tofu for 3 minutes on one side, and then use a spatula to turn it. Cook for 3 minutes on the other side. Turn the heat off and add the BBQ sauce. Move the mixture constantly around the pan so that the sugar in the sauce doesn't scorch. Once the sauce is thick and has adhered to the tofu, set the BBQ tofu aside in a medium bowl.

Roll or toss your crust into a 12-inch round. Line a pizza peel or the back of a large baking sheet with a piece of parchment paper, and place the crust onto the peel. Spread ½ cup of tomato sauce over the crust. Top that with 1 ½ cups smoked mozzarella. Place about a cup of the Chipotle BBQ Tofu over that. Finish with a cup of shredded purple cabbage. Slide the pizza with the parchment paper onto the stone. Cook for 5 to 7 minutes or until the outer crust is brown and the cheese is bubbly. Repeat the process with the remaining ingredients in order to make the second pizza.

Makes two 12-inch pizzas that will serve 6 to 8.

ARTICHOKE HEARTS AND SUCCOTASH OVER SMOKED CHEDDAR GRITS

We set out to make a vegetarian version of Creole shrimp and grits that's just as good as the original. The artichoke hearts are a perfect stand-in for the shrimp since they are region-appropriate. Each component is wonderful on its own: the smokiness of the Cheddar grits, the spicy heat of the vegetables, the crunch of the artichoke. The dish comes together with a simple mustard sauce.

2 cups vegetable stock	Cheddar cheese	(recipe follows)
2 cups 2% milk	1 teaspoon sea salt flakes	Spicy Mustard Pan Sauce
1 cup yellow corn grits	¼ teaspoon cracked	(recipe follows)
4 medium cloves	black pepper	Fresh dill (to garnish)
garlic, minced	Succotash (recipe follows)	Chopped fresh parsley
2 cups shredded smoked	Panfried Artichoke Hearts	(to garnish)

Bring the stock and milk to a boil together in a saucepan. Add the grits slowly as you stir so that there are no lumps. Add the garlic, cover, and allow the mixture to cook on low for 20 minutes. Stir occasionally to prevent sticking. Stir in the Cheddar, salt, and pepper.

Prepare the remaining components. To serve, spoon a cup of grits onto a warmed plate. Top with a ½ cup of succotash and three pieces of panfried artichoke. Drizzle a spoonful of Spicy Mustard Pan Sauce around the plate. Garnish with fresh dill and chopped parsley to taste.

Makes 4 servings.

SUCCOTASH

1 tablespoon unsalted butter	½ cup okra (¼-inch slices)	1 teaspoon paprika
1 tablespoon canola oil	½ cup fresh or prepared peas	¼ teaspoon garlic powder
1 medium ear of corn,	(field peas or lady peas)	¼ teaspoon nutmeg
kernels cut away	1 cup shallots (small dice)	¼ teaspoon iodized sea salt
1 medium green bell	Scant dash of cayenne	¼ teaspoon cracked
pepper, diced	pepper	black pepper

Heat the butter and oil in a large frying pan over medium-high heat. Toss together the corn, pepper, okra, peas, shallots, cayenne, paprika, garlic powder, nutmeg, salt, and pepper in a large bowl. Once the butter and oil begin to smoke, add the vegetable mixture. Allow it to cook for

continued next page ▸

a minute, and then stir the mixture. Allow it to cook for another minute, and then toss it again. Remove the vegetables from the pan but leave any charred bits that are stuck to the bottom of the pan for the Spicy Mustard Pan Sauce.

Makes 2 cups.

SPICY MUSTARD PAN SAUCE

¾ cup vegetable stock

1 tablespoon Creole mustard

Add the stock and mustard to the pan used to cook the succotash. Using a wooden spoon scrape up any bits that are stuck to the bottom of the pan. Over medium heat reduce the sauce by half.

Makes ⅓ to ½ cup.

PANFRIED ARTICHOKE HEARTS

There are several options when choosing artichoke hearts. We like to break down fresh artichokes or use the large ones from the olive bar. You may also use frozen or canned artichokes. They will all work in this recipe.

⅓ cup canola oil

3 quartered artichoke hearts (12 pieces)

1 large egg, beaten

½ cup all-purpose flour

Sea salt flakes and cracked black pepper (to taste)

In a 10-inch frying pan over medium-high heat, heat the oil until it shimmers. Toss the artichoke hearts in the egg and then in the flour. Shake off any excess flour. Panfry the artichoke hearts for 2 minutes per side or until golden brown. Add salt and pepper to taste.

Makes 2 servings.

Vegetarian "Chicken" with Parsley and
Olive Oil Dumplings (page 146)

VEGETARIAN "CHICKEN" WITH PARSLEY AND OLIVE OIL DUMPLINGS

Our grandmothers made chicken and dumplings all the time like it was nothing. One would appreciate a little begging before she got out the flour and milk; the other shrugged and made just dumplings after three of the grandkids went vegetarian at the same time. We adore our sweet grandmothers, and we got a huge part of our love of cooking from them. This is a dish that really brings us back.

- 2 tablespoons unsalted butter
- 1 package "chicken-style" seitan, torn into bite-size bits
- 1 cup plus 2 tablespoons all-purpose flour, divided
- ½ teaspoon of garlic powder
- ½ teaspoon cracked black pepper
- 6 cups vegetable stock
- 2 tablespoons baking powder
- 1 teaspoon plus ⅛ teaspoon iodized sea salt, divided
- ¼ cup minced fresh flat-leaf parsley, divided
- 2 tablespoons plus 1 teaspoon olive oil, divided
- ½ cup 2 % milk
- ½ cup diced carrot
- ½ cup diced celery
- ½ teaspoon champagne vinegar
- ⅛ teaspoon cane sugar

In a large soup pot or Dutch oven, melt 2 tablespoons of butter over medium-high heat. In a medium bowl toss the seitan with the 2 tablespoons of flour, and then sear the seitan in the butter until crispy and brown. After 3 minutes turn the seitan once, and brown the other side for 3 minutes. Add the garlic powder and pepper. Pour the stock over the seitan. Whisk out any floury lumps, and reduce the heat to low. Bring the stock up to a slow boil.

In a medium bowl whisk together the baking powder, 1 cup of flour, and 1 teaspoon of salt. Add 2 tablespoons parsley, 2 tablespoons olive oil, and the milk to the flour mixture. Stir just enough to mix because if you stir too much, the dumplings will become tough.

Drop the dumpling batter into the stock 1 tablespoon at a time. (You should have 10 to 12 dumplings.) Place a lid on the soup pot and reduce the heat to simmer for 15 minutes without disturbing the pot. During this time the dumplings will plump and the sauce will thicken. It's a little Southern magic.

While the dumplings cook, toss the carrot, celery, and remaining 2 tablespoons parsley with the remaining 1 teaspoon olive oil, champagne vinegar, sugar, and ⅛ teaspoon sea salt in a small bowl. Mix to incorporate. To serve, spoon three dumplings and a few pieces of seitan along with some broth into a soup bowl. Garnish with the fresh vegetable mixture.

Makes 4 to 6 servings.

DIRTY FRIED RICE, KING OYSTER MUSHROOM "SCALLOPS," AND CREOLE COCONUT SAUCE

The king oyster mushroom "scallop" may be The Chubby Vegetarian's most famous dish. It has been served in two of Memphis's finest restaurants, Andrew Michael Italian Kitchen and Acre.

We took the classic flavor of New Orleans-style dirty rice and made it into fried rice for the base of this dish. This part alone is great for a light meal or lunch, but adding the wonderfully meaty King Oyster Mushroom "Scallops" and the rich Creole Coconut Sauce on top make it unique.

King oyster mushrooms are easy to find in the produce department, or just visit the nearest Asian grocery since they carry huge king oyster mushrooms.

Dirty Fried Rice
  (recipe follows)

1 pound king oyster mushrooms

1 (13.5-ounce) can light coconut milk

1 teaspoon Old Bay Seasoning

1 tablespoon unsalted butter

1 tablespoon canola oil

Sea salt flakes and cracked black pepper (to taste)

1 tablespoon Creole mustard

1 medium clove garlic, minced or grated

Celery leaves (to garnish)

Fresh thyme (to garnish)

First, prepare Dirty Fried Rice according to the recipe on the following page.

Cut the king oyster mushrooms into ¾-inch rounds to resemble sea scallops. You should end up with about 15 slices. Place the slices into a medium dish or a bowl and cover them with coconut milk. The richness of the coconut milk is essential to the flavor and texture of this dish. Allow the mushroom slices to marinate in the coconut milk for at least 20 minutes and up to an hour.

Take the mushrooms out of the coconut milk and lay them on a clean dish towel. Reserve 1 cup of the coconut milk to be used in the sauce. Dry both sides of the mushroom and sprinkle generously with Old Bay Seasoning to taste. Heat a 10-inch frying pan over medium-high heat. Add the butter and oil. Once the butter has melted, cook the mushrooms in two batches. Sear each side for 3 minutes or until browned. Drain the mushrooms on a paper towel. Sprinkle each mushroom with salt and pepper to taste. Pour off excess fat from the pan, but don't scrape out the bits of brown stuck to the bottom of the pan. Immediately add the reserved cup of coconut milk, mustard, and garlic. Stir with a whisk over medium heat until heated through.

To assemble the dish, place 1 ½ cups Dirty Fried Rice on a plate and top with three mushroom scallops and a tablespoon of the Creole coconut sauce. Garnish with celery leaves and fresh thyme.

Makes 4 servings.

DIRTY FRIED RICE

2 cups vegetable broth

1 tablespoon tomato paste

1 cup white rice (like jasmine rice)

½ cup diced celery

½ cup diced carrot

½ cup diced shallots

¼ cup dry-packed sun-dried tomato (small dice)

1 cup diced button mushrooms (about 5)

½ teaspoon garlic powder

½ teaspoon dried thyme

½ teaspoon crushed red pepper flakes

½ teaspoon dried sage

Scant ⅛ teaspoon clove powder

¼ teaspoon liquid smoke

3 tablespoons canola oil

2 large eggs, beaten

2 tablespoons soy sauce

In a large soup pot, bring the broth and tomato paste up to a boil. Add the rice, cover the pot, and reduce the heat to low. Allow it to cook for 20 minutes. Remove the lid and allow the rice to cool completely, or just make the rice the night before to save time. (Cooling the rice will take another 20 minutes—if you try to make fried rice with warm rice, you will end up with a gummy mess!)

In a large bowl toss together the celery, carrot, shallots, sun-dried tomato, mushrooms, garlic powder, thyme, crushed red pepper flakes, sage, clove, and liquid smoke. If you have a wok, now is the time to use it. Place the wok (or your largest frying pan) over high heat. Allow the wok to get hot without anything in it. This should take 3 minutes. Add the canola oil. Once it starts to smoke, gently pour the beaten egg into the hot oil; this is cool to watch. Once it is almost dry (this takes only a few seconds), add the vegetable mixture and toss it around the pan using a large serving spoon. Use the spoon to break the egg up as you stir. Allow the vegetables to cook for 3 minutes or until they start to take on some color. Add the rice, mix it all up, and add the soy sauce. Cook another 3 minutes or until everything is heated through. Remove from the heat and cover with a large lid to keep the rice warm while you cook the other components of the dish.

Makes about 4 cups.

VEGETARIAN BOUDIN SAUSAGE

A vegetarian blood sausage sounds absurd, and sure, it is a little crazy. However, we're taking inspiration from the original, not attempting to recreate it. Traditionally, boudin, a regional New Orleans ingredient, is more like a rice and sausage casserole stuffed into a casing. So it makes perfect sense to take the spices and the texture of the rice and add another savory flavor. Here, smoked sun-dried tomatoes—not pork— provide the umami for this dish.

Serve it like a hot dog on a French roll with sautéed onions and green peppers. Add our N'awlins Sauce (page 89) and some celery leaves to garnish.

2 tablespoons canola oil	½ teaspoon smoked paprika	¼ cup chopped fresh parsley
1 cup diced onion	½ teaspoon granulated garlic	2 cups smoked sun-dried
½ cup diced celery	½ teaspoon dried oregano	tomatoes* (dry-packed)
½ teaspoon dried thyme	Sea salt flakes and cracked	1 cup cooked white rice
½ teaspoon crushed	black pepper (to taste)	¾ cup vital wheat gluten
red pepper flakes	¼ cup white wine (like	
	Pinot Grigio)	

Heat the canola oil in a medium pan over medium heat. Add the onion and celery to the pan. Cook until the onion is translucent and beginning to brown. Add the thyme, red pepper flakes, paprika, garlic, oregano, salt, and pepper. Add the wine and allow the mixture to reduce until most of the liquid has evaporated.

Remove the pan from the heat and place the cooked vegetables into the work bowl of a food processor. Add the parsley and sun-dried tomatoes. Pulse the mixture 8 to 10 times or until it's finely chopped yet still distinct. Place the mixture into a large bowl along with the cooked rice and vital wheat gluten. Mix it all vigorously by hand for at least 2 minutes.

Pull out six pieces of foil in 4-inch sections. Place a ½-cup portion (for smaller sausages, use ¼ cup) on each foil, and form it roughly into a log shape. (No need to be too precise.) Roll the foil into a tube and twist the ends. Each sausage should be 4–5 inches long. Repeat the process until all the mixture has been used. Place the foil-wrapped sausages into a steamer basket, and steam them for 45 minutes. (Our steamer is just a metal colander that fits nicely into a stock pot.) They will plump and take shape when steamed. Remove the sausages and allow them to cool completely.

When you're ready to serve, brush each sausage with canola oil before grilling. Grill on high for 2 minutes per side or until well-marked. Serve on a warm French roll with sautéed peppers and onions, plenty of N'awlins Sauce (page 89), and celery leaves for garnish.

Makes 6 large sausages.

*Smoke regular sun-dried tomatoes for 4 minutes using our Quick-Smoking Method (page 231) or buy them pre-smoked or add 1 teaspoon of liquid smoke just before adding in the wheat gluten.

SMOKED CHEDDAR JALAPEÑO CORNBREAD

The worst insult that anyone can give your cornbread in the South is that it's "just a little dry." No one will ever say that about our version. It's packed with good stuff like buttermilk, local honey, and best of all, smoked Cheddar.

1 cup cornmeal

1 cup all-purpose flour

1 teaspoon baking powder

½ teaspoon iodized sea salt

1 cup smoked Cheddar cheese

2 tablespoons minced jalapeño (1 large; optional)

¼ cup plus 1 tablespoon unsalted butter, divided

2 tablespoons honey

2 eggs, beaten

1 cup buttermilk

Place a 10-inch cast-iron skillet into a cold oven. Preheat the oven to 400 degrees F. In a large bowl mix together the cornmeal, all-purpose flour, baking powder, salt, Cheddar cheese, and jalapeño. In a medium bowl melt ¼ cup of the butter. Add the honey, eggs, and buttermilk to the melted butter and whisk the ingredients together.

Next, combine the flour mixture and egg mixture. Stir until just incorporated. Using a sturdy, reliable oven mitt, carefully remove the hot cast-iron skillet from the oven and place it onto a trivet. Place the remaining tablespoon of butter into the skillet and swirl it, or use a silicone brush to coat the bottom of the pan. Pour the batter into the pan and place the pan into the oven for 20 minutes or until the cornbread is golden brown. Run a knife around the edge and turn the cornbread out onto a cutting board. Serve hot with beans and black-eyed peas, or use it to make croutons.

Makes 4 to 6 servings.

VEGETARIAN MEATBALLS

This recipe makes use of our very versatile Mushroom Meat (page 230). This is the stuff we use in place of ground beef in any recipe in order to vegetarian-ize it, and it's more natural than commercially available ground beef substitutes. These meatballs made with Mushroom Meat are a hit over and over again in our house. We usually serve them on top of spaghetti, but they also make a great little vegetarian appetizer for a party, or you can stuff them inside of a hoagie for a vegetarian meatball sub sandwich.

1 cup shredded
    Parmesan cheese

1 cup bread crumbs

2 cups Mushroom
    Meat (page 230)

2 large eggs, beaten

1 tablespoon tomato paste

½ cup half and half

½ teaspoon red pepper
    flakes (less if you
    don't like it spicy)

½ teaspoon minced
    fresh oregano

2 tablespoons minced
    fresh parsley

2 tablespoons olive oil
    (for drizzling)

½ cup of Vegetable-Packed
    Tomato Sauce (page
    229) (for basting)

In a large bowl combine the cheese, bread crumbs, Mushroom Meat, eggs, tomato paste, half and half, red pepper flakes, oregano, and parsley. Allow the mixture to stand for 20 minutes so that the bread crumbs soak up the flavor of the other ingredients. Preheat your oven to 350 degrees F. Using a small spring-loaded ice-cream scoop (about 1 tablespoon), scoop a portion of the mixture onto a parchment-lined, 17 x 12-inch rimmed baking sheet. Portion them fairly close together as this makes a whole bunch of little meatballs. Repeat until all the mixture has been used. Drizzle the meatballs with olive oil. Place the pan in the oven. After 10 minutes take the pan out and brush the tops of the meatballs with tomato sauce. Return the pan to the oven to finish cooking the meatballs for another 10 minutes.

Makes about 36 small meatballs.

NOTE: Freeze unused meatballs on a baking sheet. Once they are frozen solid, pack them into a food storage container. They will keep up to 6 months in the freezer.

TOFU ALMONDINE IN A WHITE WINE-BUTTER SAUCE

We recently asked our readers if they liked tofu or not. Overwhelmingly, the answer was that it really depended on how it's prepared. This recipe would pass the test—the tofu is accompanied by sweet toasted almonds and a buttery white wine sauce. What could be better than this vegetarian take on a New Orleans classic?

The sauce is the key to the deliciousness of this dish. At first we used it sparingly. However, the pan with the sauce in it always finds its way to the dinner table where it is drizzled with abandon.

½ cup sliced, unsalted almonds

1 block extra-firm tofu

¼ teaspoon sea salt flakes

¼ teaspoon cracked black pepper

¼ teaspoon crushed red pepper flakes

¼ teaspoon paprika

2 tablespoons canola oil

1 tablespoon unsalted butter

¼ cup all-purpose flour

White Wine-Butter Sauce (recipe follows)

1 tablespoon chopped fresh parsley (to garnish)

Place the almonds in a dry medium pan. Toast them, stirring often, on medium-high until lightly browned. Set aside.

Cut the tofu into six triangles. Season both sides of the tofu with sea salt, cracked black pepper, red pepper flakes, and paprika to taste.

Heat a 12-inch skillet to medium heat, and add the canola and butter. Place the flour on a large dinner plate. Dredge each filet on both sides and then shake off any excess flour. Once the butter has melted, gently lay the seasoned, dredged tofu filet into the pan; this is best done in batches of three. Cook the tofu for 4 minutes on the first side until golden brown. Flip each piece and repeat the same cooking process for the other side. Remove the cooked tofu filets to a baking sheet, and keep them warm in a 300-degree F. oven until ready to serve.

To serve, place one tofu filet on a bed of wilted greens or grits, drizzle a teaspoon of White Wine-Butter Sauce over it, and then add a few toasted almonds. Repeat by stacking the filets three high. To finish, drizzle the sauce around the plate. Garnish with chopped parsley.

Makes 2 servings.

WHITE WINE-BUTTER SAUCE

3 tablespoons unsalted
  butter, divided

½ cup shallots, diced

1 lemon

2 tablespoons vegetarian
  Worcestershire sauce

1 teaspoon cane sugar

2 dried bay leaves

⅛ teaspoon cracked
  black pepper

½ cup white wine (like
  Pinot Grigio)

½ cup half and half

In a medium-size saucepan over medium heat, melt 2 tablespoons of butter and sauté the shallots until they appear translucent. This should take 3 minutes. Cut the lemon in half and add the juice from the lemon and also the rind to the pan. (Don't worry about seeds; you will strain this sauce later.) Add the Worcestershire sauce, sugar, bay leaves, pepper, and wine to the pan. Allow the mixture to reduce by half. This should take 8 minutes or so. It will look syrupy when it's properly reduced.

Turn off the heat. Temper the half and half by adding 2 tablespoons of the wine mixture to it before adding it all back into the mixture. This will keep your sauce from breaking. Strain the sauce through a fine-mesh strainer. Rinse the pan of any debris, and then return the strained sauce to the pan. Keep warm until ready to serve. Just before serving, whisk in the remaining tablespoon of butter. This process is known as mounting a sauce with butter, and it results in a very rich and flavorful sauce.

Makes 1 cup.

RATATOUILLE NAPOLEON

We didn't just put two crazy words together to get your attention. Honestly, this has become one of our favorite things to make. It would be great for a party since you can prepare everything ahead of time and then just stack it on the plates. With the salty kick of the olive tapenade and the deep flavor of the roasted vegetables, you get immense complexity. The balsamic reduction pulls it all together and turns up the volume of the whole dish.

- 1 medium-size eggplant, peeled and diced (2 to 3 cups)
- 1 cup diced white onion (about 1 medium)
- 1 green bell pepper, diced (about ½ cup)
- 1 red bell pepper, diced (about ½ cup)
- 10 ounces crimini mushrooms, diced
- 2 tablespoons olive oil, plus more for brushing on phyllo
- 2 tablespoons balsamic vinegar
- Sea salt flakes (to taste)
- Cracked black pepper (to taste)
- 8 sheets phyllo dough
- Olive Tapenade (recipe follows)
- 6 ounces ricotta cheese
- Balsamic Reduction (recipe follows)

Preheat your oven to 400 degrees F. Spread the eggplant, onion, peppers, and mushrooms onto a 17 x 9-inch rimmed baking sheet, drizzle with olive oil and balsamic vinegar, sprinkle with salt and pepper, and bake for 8 minutes or until the vegetables start to caramelize on the edges. Remove the pan from the oven and toss vegetables. Place pan back in oven for another 8 minutes. Remove the pan and allow the vegetables to cool.

Brush every other sheet of phyllo pastry with olive oil and begin to stack the sheets. Using a pizza cutter, slice the phyllo into 2 x 2-inch squares. Lay them out onto a parchment-lined baking sheet. Using a medium ice-cream scoop, transfer a generous ¼ cup of ratatouille to half of the phyllo squares. Bake the squares for 20 minutes or until the phyllo is golden. Slather the phyllo squares that are without ratatouille with a tablespoon of olive tapenade.

To serve place a spoonful of ricotta cheese in the center of the plate, stack an olive tapenade phyllo on top of the cheese, and finish the stack with the ratatouille phyllo. Finally, drizzle a tablespoon of Balsamic Reduction on top.

Makes 4 servings.

OLIVE TAPENADE

1 teaspoon olive oil	3 medium cloves garlic, chopped	½ teaspoon minced fresh oregano
½ cup minced shallots		1 cup pitted kalamata olives

In a medium pan heat the olive oil and sauté the shallots, garlic, and oregano until soft and cooked through, about 2 minutes. In a food processor blend the olives with the garlic mixture until smooth.

Makes about 1 ½ cups.

BALSAMIC REDUCTION

¼ cup balsamic vinegar	1 teaspoon cane sugar	Cracked black pepper (to taste)
½ cup white wine (like Pinot Grigio)	⅛ teaspoon sea salt flakes	3 sprigs of thyme (to garnish)

Mix the vinegar, wine, sugar, salt, pepper, and thyme in a medium saucepan. Reduce the mixture over medium heat until thick and syrupy, which takes 10 minutes.

Makes about ¾ cup.

Vegan Peanut Chili with Charred Corn
and Avocado Salsa (page 162)

VEGAN PEANUT CHILI WITH CHARRED CORN AND AVOCADO SALSA

This chili gets depth from a multitude of sources: smoky chipotle chili powder, soy sauce, and espresso. The texture, which so many vegetarian chilis lack, comes from chopped peanuts. This also adds a nice touch of protein to the dish.

The Charred Corn and Avocado Salsa is the perfect bit of chill as you chow on this spicy chili. Try it on its own for a quick appetizer at a party, or add fresh, chopped jalapeño for a little kick.

1 tablespoon olive oil

1 ½ cups diced onion

5 cloves garlic, minced

1 teaspoon ancho chili powder

1 teaspoon cumin

1 tablespoon smoked paprika

½ teaspoon chipotle chili powder

½ teaspoon garlic powder

1 cup white wine (like Pinot Grigio) or beer

1 ½ cups diced green bell peppers

1 tablespoon soy sauce

¼ cup espresso (or strong coffee)

1 tablespoon vegetarian Worcestershire sauce

1 cup chopped roasted unsalted peanuts

2 cups chopped tomatoes

3 cups vegetable stock

4 tablespoons tomato paste

1 teaspoon white vinegar

2 teaspoons light brown sugar

1 cup dry pinto beans (soaked overnight in 3 cups water)

Prepared white or brown rice

Charred Corn and Avocado Salsa (page 233); to garnish

In a Dutch oven or heavy soup pot over medium-high heat, add the olive oil, onion, and garlic. Cook for 5 minutes or until the onion is translucent. Add the ancho chili powder, cumin, smoked paprika, chipotle chili powder, and garlic powder. Stir to incorporate the spices and then deglaze the pot with the wine or beer. Allow the mixture to reduce until most of the liquid has evaporated. Add the green peppers, soy sauce, espresso, Worcestershire, peanuts, tomatoes, vegetable stock, tomato paste, vinegar, brown sugar, and pinto beans to the mix. Stir and bring to a boil. Reduce the heat to low, cover, and allow the chili to cook for 1 ½ hours or until the beans are tender.

To serve, add ½ cup of rice to a bowl followed by a ladleful of Peanut Chili. Top with ½ cup Charred Corn and Avocado Salsa.

Makes 6 servings.

PORCINI AND PORTOBELLO MUSHROOM BOURGUIGNON OVER SMASHED POTATOES

A French-vegetarian alliance is always a hit. We sometimes get ambitious and put together an all-out vegetarian French food extravaganza, and the main attraction is always this version of the French classic, boeuf bourguignon, made vegetarian with mushrooms and a very "beefy" broth consisting of red wine and porcini mushrooms. Serve this dish over some crispy-on-the-outside, creamy-on-the-inside smashed fingerling potatoes.

The bourguignon has a lot of steps but is actually simple to make. Set some time aside on a weekend day to make this vegetarian version of a comfort food classic. It's shockingly full of flavor, and even the leftovers are great.

15 to 20 pearl onions

5 large portobello mushroom caps, cut into large chunks

Sea salt flakes and cracked black pepper (to taste)

3 tablespoons olive oil or unsalted butter, divided

5 large carrots, cut into large chunks

⅓ cup French lentils

Porcini Mushroom Broth (recipe follows)

1 tablespoon all-purpose flour

12 Smashed New Potatoes (recipe follows)

¼ cup chopped fresh parsley (to garnish)

Toss the onions onto a hot gas grill until the outer skin is nice and charred on all sides; this should take only a few minutes per side. Remove and place into a covered container to cool. Once cool, the onions will slip right out of their charred skin.

Season the mushrooms with salt and pepper to taste. In a Dutch oven over medium-high heat, melt 2 tablespoons of butter or oil and then sear the mushroom chunks until nicely browned. (This is best done in batches as to not overcrowd the pan.) Remove the mushrooms and set aside in the fridge. You will add them back to the pot later.

Add the carrots and onions to the pot. Once they begin to brown, add the lentils and enough of the Porcini Mushroom Broth to cover. Stir. Put a lid on it and reduce to a simmer for 1 ½ hours. Remove the vegetables from the broth and set aside with the mushrooms.

Crank the heat up to high to reduce the broth by one-third. Remove the reduced broth from the pot and set aside in a heat-proof bowl. Check the broth for seasoning and adjust. Add the flour and remaining tablespoon of butter to the pot. Allow the mixture to cook until nutty and fragrant. Add the broth back to the pot with the roux. Mix with a whisk to work out any lumps. Bring to a boil and then reduce the heat. The sauce should look velvety and slightly thick. Add the mushrooms and vegetables back to the pot and coat them with the velvety sauce. Bring everything up to temperature just before serving. Serve over the Smashed Potatoes and garnish with parsley.

Makes 4 servings.

PORCINI MUSHROOM BROTH

1 medium white onion

3 tablespoons olive oil

2 medium carrots

6 ribs celery

1 ounce dried porcini
   mushrooms

1 cup loose-packed
   fresh parsley

6 sprigs fresh thyme

Juice of ½ lemon

2 bay leaves

1 teaspoon cane sugar

1 teaspoon sea salt flakes

1 tablespoon tomato paste

2 cups dry red wine
   (like Burgundy)

3 cups water

Process the onion in a food processor until it's finely chopped. In a stock pot over medium-high heat, heat the olive oil and then sweat the onions in the oil until they are translucent. Process the carrots and celery in the same way and add them to the pot. Add the dried mushrooms and the parsley, thyme, lemon juice, bay leaves, sugar, salt, tomato paste, red wine, and water to the pot and bring to a simmer. Reduce the heat, cover, and allow the mixture to cook for 25 minutes. Strain out all the vegetables and discard them. Return the stock to the stovetop with the heat on high and reduce by about a third.

Makes 2 ½ to 3 cups.

SMASHED NEW POTATOES

12 medium new potatoes

¼ cup canola oil

Sea salt flakes and cracked
   black pepper (to taste)

Preheat your oven to 350 degrees F. Bake the new potatoes for 20 minutes. Remove them and allow them to cool. With the bottom of a frying pan, smash the potatoes hard enough to flatten them. Heat the canola oil over medium-high heat in a 10-inch frying pan and then panfry the smashed potatoes about 3 minutes per side. You just need to crisp the outside since the potato is already cooked through. Remove the potatoes and drain them on paper towels. Sprinkle with salt and pepper.

Makes 4 servings.

VEGETARIAN MEATLOAF WITH GARLIC MASHED POTATOES

As you probably could've guessed, our meatloaf features the meaty texture and savory flavor of mushrooms. We also add tempeh and walnuts for their flavor and hearty texture. This loaf is tender and delicious, especially when it's served over Garlic Mashed Potatoes and topped with a Parsley and Tomato Salad.

In the unlikely event of leftovers, there's nothing better than a few slices of vegetarian meatloaf dressed with mashed potatoes and Cheddar cheese between two slices of sourdough bread.

2 tablespoons unsalted butter

2 cups finely chopped onion (about 1 medium)

½ cup finely chopped celery (about 2 ribs)

½ cup finely chopped carrot (about 2 medium)

2 vegetarian bouillon cubes

8 ounces crimini (baby bella) mushrooms, finely chopped

½ cup diced green bell pepper (about 1 medium)

1 block tempeh, crumbled

1 cup smoked sun-dried tomatoes*, finely chopped

1 cup walnuts, finely chopped

¼ cup ketchup

1 teaspoon English mustard (or yellow mustard)

1 cup bread crumbs

2 eggs, beaten

½ teaspoon garlic powder

¼ teaspoon crushed red pepper flakes

½ teaspoon dried thyme

1 teaspoon paprika

¼ cup half and half

Ketchup Glaze (recipe follows)

Garlic Mashed Potatoes (recipe follows)

Parsley and Tomato Salad (recipe follows)

Preheat your oven to 350 degrees F. Melt the butter in a 12-inch skillet over medium-high heat. Add the onion, celery, and carrot to the pan and stir. Cook until the onion is translucent and beginning to brown, about 10 minutes. Add the bouillon cubes and stir into the vegetable mixture until incorporated.

Place the mixture into a large bowl. Add the mushroom, bell pepper, tempeh, sun-dried tomatoes, walnuts, ketchup, mustard, bread crumbs, eggs, garlic powder, red pepper flakes, thyme, paprika, and half and half. Work the mixture together with your hands until everything is well incorporated. Allow the mixture to rest in the fridge for 10 minutes.

On a parchment-lined 17 x 12-inch rimmed baking sheet, place the mixture in the center. Using your hands, form a loaf that's approximately 12 inches long, 6 inches wide, and 2 ½ inches tall. The loaf should be smooth and have rounded edges. This will help it stay together when serving.

Place the loaf in the oven for 25 minutes. While the meatloaf is baking, prepare the Ketchup Glaze, the Garlic Mashed Potatoes and the Parsley and Tomato Salad.

Brush the loaf with the Ketchup Glaze, and return the loaf to the oven for another 10 minutes; brush another coat of glaze on top, and bake for a final 10 minutes.

To serve, place a generous spoonful of Garlic Mashed Potatoes in the center of a plate, top with a slice of Vegetarian Meatloaf, and finish with a touch of the Parsley and Tomato Salad.

Makes 8 servings.

*If you cannot find smoked sun-dried tomatoes, just use plain sun-dried tomatoes and add a teaspoon of liquid smoke to the meatloaf mix, or make your own using our Quick-Smoking Method (page 231).

NOTE: *When preparing your vegetables, it's good to note that a majority of the work may be done in the food processor. Just add your roughly chopped ingredients and pulse the processor a few times until they are all broken down and become finely chopped. This works particularly well with the onion, celery, and carrots. The other ingredients are best chopped by hand.*

KETCHUP GLAZE

½ cup organic ketchup	¼ teaspoon hot sauce	1 tablespoon sorghum (or maple syrup)
1 tablespoon soy sauce	1 teaspoon cracked black pepper	

Mix the ketchup, soy sauce, hot sauce, black pepper, and sorghum until well incorporated and set aside.

Makes about ⅔ cup.

GARLIC MASHED POTATOES

5 cups peeled, diced potatoes (like Idaho or Yukon Gold)	1 cup half and half	¼ teaspoon cracked black pepper
2 cups chopped cauliflower	8 medium cloves garlic, chopped	¼ cup sour cream
1 ½ tablespoons unsalted butter	½ teaspoon sea salt flakes	

Place the potatoes, cauliflower, butter, half and half, garlic, salt, and pepper in a covered, microwave-safe dish. Microwave on high for 12 minutes. Mash with a potato masher, and then add the sour cream.

Makes about 8 cups.

PARSLEY AND TOMATO SALAD

1 ½ cups diced tomato
    (1 large)

½ cup chopped fresh parsley

¼ cup diced shallots

⅛ teaspoon sea salt flakes

⅛ teaspoon cracked
    black pepper

⅛ teaspoon cane sugar

1 teaspoon champagne
    vinegar

Toss the tomato, parsley, shallots, salt, pepper, sugar, and vinegar together in a small bowl and set aside in the refrigerator.

Makes about 2 ¼ cups.

Vegetarian Red Beans and Rice with
Andouille Eggplant (page 170)

VEGETARIAN RED BEANS AND RICE WITH ANDOUILLE EGGPLANT

We've been making vegetarian red beans and rice for a long, long time, but this is the best version yet. The tasty addition of the andouille-spiced eggplant and smoky sun-dried tomatoes is something we wish we'd thought of long ago. This is a great recipe for entertaining because everything can be done well ahead of time. In fact, it tastes even better the next day. Serve with some crunchy, buttered French bread and a healthy dash of hot sauce.

2 tablespoons
  unsalted butter

2 tablespoons canola oil

2 cups diced onion

1 cup diced celery

1 cup diced green bell pepper

1 cup diced smoked sun-
  dried tomatoes*

4 cloves garlic, minced

½ teaspoon garlic powder

⅛ teaspoon cayenne pepper

1 teaspoon paprika

½ teaspoon dried thyme

1 tablespoon Creole mustard

1 teaspoon red miso
  paste (optional)

1 ½ cups dried red beans
  (soaked overnight in
  3 cups of water)

4 cups vegetable stock

2 tablespoons white vinegar

2 bay leaves

Sea salt flakes and cracked
  black pepper (to taste)

1 ½ cups water

6 cups cooked brown rice

Andouille Eggplant
  (recipe follows)

½ cup sliced green
  onion (to garnish)

Hot sauce (to garnish)

Heat the butter and oil in a Dutch oven over medium-high heat. Add the onion and sweat it down until it is translucent and beginning to brown. Add the celery, green pepper, smoked sun-dried tomatoes, and fresh garlic. Cook until all the vegetables begin to soften, about 8 minutes. Stir in the garlic powder, cayenne, paprika, thyme, mustard, and miso. Add the soaked and drained beans, stock, vinegar, bay leaves, salt, and pepper. Allow the mixture to simmer over low heat for 2 hours or until the beans are tender. Add water if the mixture looks dry—the liquid should be above the beans by at least an inch.

To serve, spoon a cup of rice onto the center of a dinner plate and add an equal amount of the red bean mixture on top. Top that with slices of Andouille Eggplant. Garnish with sliced green onion and plenty of hot sauce.

Makes 8 servings.

*If smoked sun-dried tomatoes are unavailable in your area, simply use sun-dried tomatoes and a teaspoon of liquid smoke, or make your own using our Quick-Smoking Method (page 231).

ANDOUILLE EGGPLANT

½ teaspoon sea salt flakes

½ teaspoon dried thyme

½ teaspoon garlic powder

½ teaspoon crushed
red pepper flakes

½ teaspoon cracked
black pepper

3 tablespoons canola
oil, divided

4 cups Japanese eggplant,
sliced 1-inch thick

In a large bowl or bag combine the salt, thyme, garlic powder, red pepper, black pepper and 1 ½ tablespoons of canola oil. Toss the eggplant slices with the mixture.

Heat a large frying pan over high heat. Add the remaining canola oil to the pan. Once the oil begins to smoke, add the eggplant so that one side of each eggplant slice makes contact with the pan. Working quickly, turn each slice over once it is deeply browned, about 45 seconds, and cook the other side in the same way. This may be done in batches—just add a little canola if the pan looks dry. Set the cooked eggplant aside on a paper towel to drain.

Makes 4 servings.

MEMPHIS-STYLE DRY RUB BBQ TOFU

Memphis BBQ (including BBQ tofu) is unique for a myriad of reasons; chief among them is the dry rub we apply before the stuff makes its way to the grill. The concept seems strange, but think of it as a dry marinade. The dry rub punches up the flavor, and it also keeps the tofu from sticking to the grill grates.

This is an easy recipe to make for a crowd. Just plan for a block of tofu to feed two people and adjust the recipe accordingly. This is wonderful and easy to eat served as a sandwich, but you can also thread four or five slices of tofu onto a few bamboo skewers and create fun-to-eat "ribs" that everyone will love.

2 blocks extra-firm tofu, drained and dried	Sea salt flakes and cracked black pepper (to taste)	1 ½ cups BBQ sauce (either Chipotle BBQ Sauce, on page 226 or a good-quality bottle of spicy sauce)
4 tablespoons Memphis BBQ Dry Rub (page 225)	1 tablespoon canola oil (to oil your grill grates)	

Tofu can be tricky to grill because it stubbornly sticks to the grates. A well-oiled grill plus the dry rub will help keep the tofu intact.

Cut each block of tofu into eight equal pieces and lay them flat on a sheet pan. Generously sprinkle the dry rub, salt, and pepper over the tofu slices. Turn the slices over and repeat. Turn your gas grill on high; allow it to preheat for 10 minutes. This is imperative. If the grill is not hot, your tofu will stick.

Using a folded paper towel and tongs, oil the grill grates just before placing the tofu on the grill. Place the tofu on the grill and leave it alone for 4 minutes. Turn the tofu using your tongs and allow it to cook another 4 minutes. Line the upper rack of your grill with foil. Remove the tofu from the direct heat and onto the upper rack of your grill. Reduce the heat to medium. Using a basting brush, brush both sides of tofu with BBQ sauce. Add sauce every 10 minutes of so until you're ready to serve. The longer you leave it on the grill, the more of a crunchy crust it will have.

Makes 4 to 6 servings.

BUTTERNUT SQUASH ROTINI MAC AND CHEESE

This is a beautiful marriage of a traditional mac and cheese and a new-ish idea that has been floating around where a humble butternut squash is blended into the cheese sauce to lower the fat and calories of this notorious gut bomb. The bonus is that the butternut squash adds a nice hit of sweetness and moisture to the dish in addition to improving its stats. That's right! Adding butternut squash makes mac and cheese healthier and better. How rare and wonderful is that?

1 medium butternut squash, peeled, seeded, and cubed (5 to 6 cups)

6 garlic cloves

2 ½ cups rotini pasta

1 tablespoon unsalted butter

1 tablespoon all-purpose flour

1 cup whole milk

2 cups shredded cheese (smoked Gouda, white Cheddar, and goat)

Kosher salt and cracked black pepper, to taste

Scant ⅛ teaspoon nutmeg

½ teaspoon sherry vinegar

5 sprigs thyme, stems discarded

1 cup bread crumbs

2 to 3 tablespoons black truffle oil

Preheat your oven to 350 degrees. Bring a large pot of heavily salted water to a boil. Add the squash and garlic cloves to the boiling water and cook for 5 to 7 minutes or until very tender. Retrieve the squash and garlic from the boiling water using a spider skimmer and place into the work bowl of you food processor. Now in the same water, cook the rotini according to package instructions. Drain the water from the pasta and return the pasta to the pot. Set aside.

In a medium pan over medium heat, melt the butter and whisk in the flour. Cook until the flour starts to smell nutty and fragrant and begins to lightly brown. Add the milk, continue to whisk, turn the heat up to medium high, and allow the mixture to boil. You will notice the mixture has thickened. Stir in the cheese and remove the pan from the heat. Add the cheese mixture to the work bowl (the one with the squash) of the food processor along with the salt, pepper, nutmeg, and sherry vinegar. Blend until completely smooth.

Pour the mixture into the pot with the cooked pasta, add the thyme, and mix until well incorporated. Pour into an 8 x 12 casserole dish. (It will look like too much sauce for the amount of pasta, but it's not!) Cover with bread crumbs and drizzle with black truffle oil. Bake for 25 minutes and serve hot out of the oven.

Makes 6 servings.

TIP: Look for a butternut squash that's smooth, firm, and heavy for its size. You can peel it using a vegetable peeler and scrape the seeds out using a spoon.

DESSERTS

Grilled Peach Ice Cream   178

No-Bake Chipotle Chocolate Tart   180

Rosemary-Lemon Cookies   182

Brown Rice and Brown Butter Crispies   183

Nannie's Blueberry Pie   185

Nannie's Pound Cake   186

Bourbon Pecan Tart   188

Spicy Cucumber-Lemonade Popsicles   191

Mascarpone Banana Pudding   192

Olive Oil Shortbread with Salted Dark Chocolate Ganache   195

Strawberry-Basil Shortcake Sliders   197

Triple-Ginger Apple Crisp   200

Egg Custard Brûlée   202

GRILLED PEACH ICE CREAM

Homemade peach ice cream is always great in the summertime, but we wondered if it was possible to make this traditional Southern recipe even better. Why not grill the peaches before adding them into the cream? It's smoky, savory, and a whole different level of great. Served with slices of grilled peach, this is a must for your next summer cookout.

Special equipment:
ice cream maker

3 medium peaches,
    peeled and halved

¾ cup light brown sugar

Juice of 1 organic lemon
    (about 1 tablespoon)

1 cup heavy cream

1 teaspoon vanilla extract

⅛ teaspoon sea salt flakes

4 sprigs of fresh mint
    (to garnish)

Put the freezer bowl of the ice-cream maker in the freezer for at least 6 hours before making this dish. Over a high flame on an outdoor grill, grill the peaches cut side down until well-marked by the grill grates. You want some of the sugars to blacken. Using tongs flip the peaches and grill the other side until well-marked by the grill grates. Remove the peaches from the grill.

In the work bowl of your food processor, add the grilled peaches, brown sugar, lemon juice, heavy cream, vanilla, and salt. Blend until very smooth. Add this mixture to your ice-cream maker and prepare according to the manufacturer's instructions. (It usually takes about 20 minutes to freeze.)

Eaten immediately out of the ice-cream maker, this ice cream's texture is similar to soft-serve ice cream. You may also scrape the mixture into a food storage container and harden it in the freezer, which will give you a more scoopable consistency. Just remember to remove the ice cream from the freezer 10 minutes before serving so it's easier to scoop.

To serve, scoop a generous portion of Grilled Peach Ice Cream into a bowl. Serve alongside warm grilled peaches and a sprig of mint.

Makes 4 servings.

NO-BAKE CHIPOTLE CHOCOLATE TART

My grandmother used to make fried pies for us all the time. There was nothing better than to be sent back home from Mamaw's house with a bag full of peach, apple, plum, and my favorite, chocolate fried pies. They were so wonderfully greasy that they would make dark spots on the outside of the paper grocery sack that held them.

Why can't fried be as good for us as broccoli and cauliflower? Maybe one day. Until then, we've come up with a way to get our chocolate pie without deep frying. In fact, there is very little at all to do. This deceptively simple pie packs a big punch thanks to some rich chocolate and just a touch of smoky heat brought on by chipotle chili powder.

2 (3-ounce) chocolate bars, chopped (70% cocoa)

½ cup heavy cream

¼ teaspoon chipotle chili powder

¼ teaspoon sea salt flakes

½ cup light brown sugar

1 (12-ounce) box extra-firm silken tofu

Graham Cracker Crust, cooked and cooled (recipe follows)

In a double boiler over medium heat, whisk the chocolate and cream together until the chocolate has melted and the cream is incorporated. This takes 10 minutes. Into the work bowl of your food processor, add the chocolate mixture, along with the chipotle, salt, brown sugar, and tofu. Blend until very smooth. Spoon the mixture into the crust and smooth it. Allow the tart to chill for 2 hours in the refrigerator—no need to bake it. Serve as is or with a whipped cream or meringue topping.

Makes 6 servings.

GRAHAM CRACKER CRUST

1 sleeve honey graham crackers (1 ½ cups)

4 tablespoons cold, unsalted butter, cubed

1 tablespoon cane sugar

Preheat your oven to 350 degrees F. Place the graham crackers, butter, and sugar into the work bowl of your food processor. Pulse until finely chopped and the butter is incorporated. The mixture should look like sand.

Press the mixture into the bottom of an 11-inch tart pan. Make sure to press the crumbs into the scallops of the pan as well, until it is ½ inch up the inside wall. Bake the crust for 15 minutes. Allow it to cool completely before filling.

Makes 1 crust.

ROSEMARY-LEMON COOKIES

In the summer and even into the fall, there's so much rosemary flourishing in our garden—big, established plants that come back even stronger each spring—and sometimes it's tough to find a use for all of it since it grows so fast. The first two steps of this recipe are chopping up the leaves of a fragrant fistful of just-picked rosemary and then using your hands to mix it with sugar, salt, and lemon zest; this makes the kitchen smell amazing.

The funny thing about these is that they fall on that line between sweet and savory. It's your call: have them with milk or top them with Parmesan and enjoy a couple with a glass of wine.

1 tablespoon fresh rosemary, stems removed; finely chopped

¼ teaspoon sea salt

½ teaspoon lemon zest (from 2 lemons)

½ cup cane sugar

2 tablespoons light brown sugar

1 egg, beaten

½ cup soy or olive oil margarine, melted

1 teaspoon vanilla extract

1 ½ cups all-purpose flour

1 teaspoon baking powder

Combine the rosemary, salt, lemon zest, cane sugar, and brown sugar in a bowl and mix well using your fingers. In another bowl whisk the egg and then add the margarine and vanilla and stir. Pour in the sugar-rosemary mixture and stir. In another bowl whisk together the flour and baking powder and add this to the egg mixture. Mix until none of the flour is visible. Chill the dough in a container in the freezer for 30 minutes.

Preheat the oven to 350 degrees F. Place the chilled dough onto a lightly floured surface, flour your rolling pin, and roll out to about ¼-inch thickness. Use a cookie cutter or a glass to cut cookies. Place on 2 parchment-lined cookie sheets and bake until the edges are golden brown, about 12 minutes.

Makes 24 cookies

BROWN RICE AND BROWN BUTTER CRISPIES

We had some vegan marshmallows in a pan on the stove and accidentally scorched them by not adding the butter at the right time. It was a mess! But it smelled kind of great in a s'mores sort of way, so we went ahead and made crispies anyway. The rich and smoky effect of brown butter makes these taste even better than the ones we remember from childhood.

4 tablespoons unsalted butter	**10 ounces vegan marshmallows**	**4 ½ cups puffed brown rice cereal**
		¼ teaspoon sea salt flakes

Melt the butter in a large saucepan over medium heat, stirring constantly. Look for a toasty color, but be sure not to turn your back on it for a second. Once you see some browning and the butter becomes fragrant, take it off the heat and add in the marshmallows. Stir constantly, and put on low heat to melt. This takes at least 3 minutes. Take the pan off the heat again and add the puffed brown rice and salt. Stir until the cereal is coated. Using a folded sheet of waxed paper, press the mixture tightly into an 8 x 8-inch pan. Sprinkle the top with salt and then allow crispies to cool. Wait about 30 minutes to cut them.

Makes 12 servings.

e's Blueberry Pie

cups blueberries

c sugar

tsp. salt

flour juice

Blueberry Pie

2½ Cups Blueberries ¼ cup Flour
1 Cup Sugar 1 Tbsp. Lemon Ju
½ teasp. Salt 2 Tbsp. Butter

Combine Berries, Sugar + flour,
Salt + lemon juice Fill 8 inch
Crust. Dot with butter. Put on
Crust. Bake 450° for 10 Min, Then
@ 350° for 40 Min Or bak

NANNIE'S BLUEBERRY PIE

A very talented baker, my grandmother Nannie used to sell her pies and pound cakes every week in Mississippi and always had something amazing for us to try when we visited. There would always be a lemon-glazed, faintly coconut-flavored pound cake waiting in the Tupperware carrier on top of the fridge and a chilled blueberry pie in the fridge.

Eating this blueberry pie has been as natural to my family as breathing. It's not super-sweet, it stains everything in sight, and it must be served cold. I use a little less sugar and add more blueberries in my version, but everything else is the same.

Basic Piecrust Dough (page 227)

¼ cup all-purpose flour

3 cups fresh (or frozen) blueberries

¾ cup plus 1 tablespoon cane sugar, divided

1 teaspoon iodized sea salt

Juice of 1 lemon (about 1 tablespoon)

2 tablespoons unsalted butter, melted and divided

2 tablespoons unsalted butter, cubed

Prepare the Basic Pie Crust Dough, cover, and set it in the fridge to rest. Preheat your oven to 450 degrees F. In a large mixing bowl sift the flour over the berries and add ¾ cup sugar, salt, and lemon juice. Mix gently.

Use a silicone brush to coat an 8-inch pie pan with 1 tablespoon of melted butter. Roll one pie crust loosely around a rolling pin and then unroll it into the pie pan. Pour the blueberry mixture into the bottom crust and then dot the mixture with small cubes of butter before using the rolling-pin method again to add the top crust. Fold the edges of the top crust under the bottom crust, and use your knuckle to crimp the edges. Use a silicone brush to brush the remaining 1 tablespoon of melted butter on the top crust of the pie. Cut 5 slits in the top crust, and sprinkle a tablespoon of sugar over the top. Bake at 450 degrees F. for 10 minutes, and then lower the temperature to 350 degrees F. for 40 minutes. Let it cool, and then refrigerate it for 3 hours or overnight before cutting a slice.

Makes 6 servings.

NANNIE'S POUND CAKE

Even though I eventually hounded Nannie out of all her secret pound cake tips, such as setting the ingredients out for an hour so that they're all at room temperature and putting the cake into a cold oven and then heating it, I always know my own attempt will never measure up to the pound cake she makes.

It is the first item gone from the table at the church suppers I've attended with her. I love dessert, and in all honesty, this stands as the best dessert I have ever had.

6 tablespoons unsalted butter	¼ cup non-hydrogenated vegetable shortening	1 teaspoon vanilla extract
2 tablespoons coconut oil	3 large eggs, beaten	1 teaspoon coconut extract
4 ounces Neufchâtel cheese	1 ½ cups cane sugar	Lemon Glaze (recipe follows)
	1 ½ cups all-purpose flour	

First, measure and set out all the ingredients on the counter. Wait an hour before you begin since the butter, Neufchâtel cheese, and eggs must come to room temperature first.

In a stand mixer with the whisk attachment, beat the butter, coconut oil, Neufchâtel cheese, and shortening well. Add the eggs and beat well. Add the sugar and flour and beat well. Add the vanilla and coconut extracts and beat well. Pour the batter into a buttered loaf pan or small Bundt pan.

Put the cake in the cold oven and then heat it to 325 degrees F. Bake the cake for 1 ½ hours or until golden brown. Allow the cake to cool in the pan for 10 minutes before removing it to a cooling rack. Pour the Lemon Glaze over the warm cake, and let it set for an hour before serving.

Makes 8 servings.

LEMON GLAZE

½ cup powdered sugar	3 teaspoons 2% milk	½ teaspoon vanilla extract
½ tablespoon unsalted butter, melted	Fine zest of 1 lemon	

Whisk together the sugar, butter, milk, lemon zest, and vanilla. You want a thick-enough-to-pour consistency in the end, so add a teaspoon more milk if needed.

Makes ¼ cup.

BOURBON PECAN TART

As much as we love it, we've never made a pecan pie in our own kitchen until recently. Why not? We swore off corn syrup in any form years ago, and it's the base of most pecan pie recipes. Our pecan tart features brown rice syrup, an ingredient easily found at natural foods stores, in its place. We also added a little bourbon to keep things interesting. The result is a delicious pecan flavor that's not cloyingly sweet or overly gooey. This one is a keeper that'll definitely find its way onto your holiday dessert table. Make your own crust and whipped cream for this tart, and maybe you'll fall in love with pecan pie again too.

Basic Piecrust Dough
(page 227)

2 cups unsalted
pecans, toasted

2 large eggs, beaten

1 teaspoon vanilla extract

½ cup firm packed
light brown sugar

⅔ cup brown rice syrup

¼ teaspoon sea salt flakes

¼ cup soy or olive
oil margarine

2 tablespoons bourbon

Easy Whipped Cream (to
garnish) (recipe follows)

Preheat the oven to 350 degrees F. Make the piecrust dough and set it aside in the refrigerator. In a large bowl mix the pecans, eggs, vanilla, brown sugar, brown rice syrup, salt, margarine, and bourbon until well incorporated. Remove the dough from the refrigerator and roll it out to approximately 14 inches round. Press the dough into an 11-inch tart pan and press the edges into the scallops with your thumb. Dock the dough with a fork and par-bake it for 10 minutes. Pour the filling into the crust and smooth it with a rubber spatula. Return the tart to the oven for 30 minutes. Allow the tart to cool completely before serving. Serve with whipped cream.

Makes 1 tart that serves 6 to 8 people.

EASY WHIPPED CREAM

½ cup heavy whipping cream   1 tablespoon powdered sugar   1 teaspoon vanilla extract

In a large bowl whisk the cream vigorously until slightly stiff. Add the sugar and vanilla and whisk to combine. Set the whipped cream aside in the refrigerator until ready to serve.

Makes about 1 ½ cups.

SPICY CUCUMBER-LEMONADE POPSICLES

Cucumbers are so plentiful during the summer, and these sweet, salty, spicy popsicles make mighty fine use of them. Ancho chili and cayenne add an unexpected kick and subtle color to these.

Special equipment: popsicle molds, popsicle sticks

1 large English cucumber (about 12 inches)

Juice of 1 ½ lemons (about 1 ½ tablespoons)

Juice of ½ lime (about 1 tablespoon)

⅓ cup cane sugar

1 ½ tablespoons light agave nectar

⅛ teaspoon sea salt flakes

⅛ teaspoon ancho chili powder

Scant ⅛ teaspoon cayenne pepper

Peel the English cucumber and chop it into 3-inch pieces. Put the cucumber, lemon juice, and lime juice into a food processor, and process until the mixture appears smooth and liquid. Place a fine mesh strainer over a bowl and strain out any pulp. Press the pulp repeatedly with a silicone spatula to release all of the juice. Discard the pulp.

Whisk the juice mixture with cane sugar, agave nectar, salt, ancho chili powder, and cayenne pepper until fully combined. Pour into the popsicle molds. This recipe makes 5 pops, but it can easily be doubled. Freeze them for at least 4 hours, and then briefly run warm water over the outside of the molds for easy removal of the pops.

Makes 5 pops.

MASCARPONE BANANA PUDDING

Why not mix the richness of mascarpone into a dessert we Southerners already treasure—and put it in a jar to boot? Don't let the kitschiness fool you; this dessert is serious. The blended bananas and creamy mascarpone take on the texture of pudding, but the mixture has a richness you can't get from a box.

Special equipment:
4 small (about 1 cup)
mason jars or teacups

1 cup mascarpone cheese

3 medium bananas (two
mashed and one to slice)

1 teaspoon vanilla extract

⅛ teaspoon sea salt flakes

2 tablespoons
powdered sugar

12 vanilla wafers, crumbled
(about 1 cup)

Meringue (recipe follows)

Place the mascarpone cheese, the flesh of 2 mashed bananas, vanilla, salt, and powdered sugar into the work bowl of your food processor. Blend until completely smooth. Divide the crushed wafers among the jars, making sure they are spread evenly in order to cover the bottom of the jar. Divide the sliced banana among the jars, adding 4 slices per jar. Divide the mascarpone and banana mixture among the four jars. Leave about ½ inch of space at the top of the jar for the meringue.

Preheat your oven to 350 degrees F. Add the meringue to the top of each jar with a spoon. Pile it on to about 2 inches. Place the jars in the oven for 5 to 7 minutes or until the meringue is lightly browned. Place the warm jars in the fridge to cool for 15 minutes.

Makes 4 servings.

MERINGUE

2 large egg whites, chilled

⅛ teaspoon cream of tartar

1 tablespoon powdered sugar

1 teaspoon vanilla extract

Using your stand mixer or a medium metal bowl and a whisk, beat the cold egg whites and cream of tartar until the whites form soft peaks. This means that when you pull the whisk away from the beaten whites, the peak slowly flops over. Add the sugar and vanilla. Whisk to incorporate.

Makes about 1 ½ cups.

OLIVE OIL SHORTBREAD WITH SALTED DARK CHOCOLATE GANACHE

We love olive oil more than just about anything else in this world. It's just one of those things that makes all the annoying parts of life recede. We pour it in ribbons across the top of fruit crumbles and eat it plain with crusty bread, sea salt, and cracked black pepper.

I've made herb-infused olive oil, and I like an olive oil pie crust, but I wanted to try using this oil in a more upfront way for dessert. This shortbread has a slight savory quality, but what pushes it over the top is dipping the edges in dark chocolate ganache and then sprinkling them with sea salt flakes.

½ cup olive oil, plus 2 tablespoons, divided

½ cup powdered sugar

1 teaspoon vanilla paste

¼ teaspoon sea salt flakes, plus some for garnish

2 tablespoons cold unsalted butter (small dice)

1 ½ cups all-purpose flour

½ cup whole wheat pastry flour

Salted Dark Chocolate Ganache (recipe follows)

Using the stand mixer, combine well the ½ cup of olive oil and powdered sugar. Stop and add the vanilla paste, salt, and butter, and then mix. Switch to a low speed and add the all-purpose flour and whole wheat flour. Drizzle in the remaining 2 tablespoons of olive oil a tablespoon at a time while the mixer remains on low until the dough comes together. Wrap the dough in waxed paper and set it in the freezer for 30 minutes to chill.

Roll out the dough to a ¾-inch thickness and cut into rectangles. Poke holes into the top of each piece with a fork. Freeze the shortbread for another 30 minutes. Preheat your oven to 350 degrees F. Remove the shortbread from the freezer and bake for 8 to 10 minutes or until golden.

Allow them to cool completely before dipping them in the Salted Dark Chocolate Ganache and sprinkling them with sea salt.

Makes 24 cookies.

SALTED DARK CHOCOLATE GANACHE

⅓ cup chopped dark chocolate

1 tablespoon heavy cream

In a microwave-safe dish combine the dark chocolate and heavy cream, and then microwave for 30 seconds. Whisk the mixture.

Makes about ⅓ cup.

STRAWBERRY-BASIL SHORTCAKE SLIDERS

One Saturday in May, we procured 4 quarts of strawberries at the market; it was time to do something interesting with them, so we started dreaming. This idea came to us, and like a shortcake freight train, could not be stopped even by the threat of late-night tornadic activity, which is par for the course every Memphis spring. We ran out to pick up our basil and cream and had this dessert made and devoured before one of us fell fast asleep in the safest spot, the hallway, amongst storm sirens and wind.

And it sure was worth it.

1 cup all-purpose flour

1 tablespoon cane sugar

1 ½ teaspoons baking powder

¼ teaspoon sea salt flakes

¼ cup unsalted butter

1 large egg, beaten

⅔ cup heavy cream, divided

Basil Compound Butter
  (recipe follows)

Strawberry Jam
  (recipe follows)

1 cup strawberries (small dice)

Fresh basil (to garnish)

Preheat your oven to 450 degrees F. Sift together the flour, sugar, baking powder, and salt, and then cut in the butter until there's a coarse crumb. Add the egg and ⅓ cup of the cream, and stir gently. Use a small, 1-tablespoon ice-cream scoop to portion out hearty, mini clumps of dough onto a parchment-lined sheet pan. Bake for 8 minutes. Let the shortcakes cool for a bit, and then split them.

In a medium bowl whip the remaining ⅓ cup of the cream until it is slightly stiff, about 4 minutes. Put a small dollop of the whipped cream on the plate, and place the bottom half of the split shortcake on top. Spread ¼ teaspoon of basil butter on the shortcake, and then spread a teaspoon of warm strawberry jam. Add a teaspoon of fresh strawberries and one more dollop of the whipped cream. Place the top of the shortcake on the stack.

Garnish each slider with a small leaf or two of fresh basil.

Makes 15 small shortcakes, about 6 servings.

BASIL COMPOUND BUTTER

¼ cup loose-packed fresh basil leaves

1 ½ tablespoons unsalted butter

Mix the basil and butter in a small food processor or by mincing the basil and stirring in the butter. Set aside in fridge until you're ready to plate the shortcakes.

Makes 2 tablespoons.

STRAWBERRY JAM

2 cups sliced strawberries
⅓ cup cane sugar

**Juice from ½ lemon, and
one long strip of its peel**

Pinch of iodized sea salt

In a medium saucepan combine the strawberries, sugar, lemon juice, lemon peel, and salt. Mash with a potato masher or the back of a fork. Cook on medium-low heat for an hour or until the mixture reaches a jam-like consistency. Stir it often. Remove the peel and discard. Set aside to cool.

Makes 1 cup.

TRIPLE-GINGER APPLE CRISP

We love making this crisp because it's so easy to put together on a weekend morning or to set up the night before and refrigerate overnight before baking. Sometimes we even top it with vanilla ice cream and have it for dessert. The three kinds of ginger give it quite a spicy kick.

10 medium Granny Smith apples, peeled and sliced into small, 1-inch pieces

Juice of 1 lemon (about 1 tablespoon)

1 tablespoon minced crystallized ginger

1 tablespoon peeled, grated fresh ginger

1 tablespoon all-purpose flour

¼ cup cane sugar

¼ cup light brown sugar

Pinch of sea salt flakes

1 tablespoon soy or olive oil margarine

Oat Streusel Topping (recipe follows)

2 tablespoons olive oil

Honeyed Yogurt (recipe follows)

Preheat your oven to 375 degrees F. In a medium saucepan combine the apples and lemon juice. Add the crystallized ginger, fresh ginger, flour, cane sugar, brown sugar, and the pinch of salt. Stir to coat the apples. Cook the apple mixture in the saucepan over medium heat, stirring often, for about 20 minutes or until caramelized. Use the margarine to butter a shallow 11 x 7-inch baking dish, and then pour the filling into it.

Spread the Oat Streusel Topping across the pan of apple filling. Drizzle it with olive oil. Bake for 45 minutes or until the topping is brown and the apples bubble around the edges. Let it cool for at least 15 minutes. Top with the Honeyed Yogurt before serving.

Makes 6 servings.

OAT STREUSEL TOPPING

1 cup rolled oats

¼ cup whole wheat flour

¼ cup all-purpose flour

½ teaspoon powdered ginger

⅛ teaspoon nutmeg

½ teaspoon cinnamon

½ teaspoon sea salt flakes (plus more for sprinkling)

⅓ cup soy or olive oil margarine

In a large bowl combine the oats, whole wheat flour, all-purpose flour, powdered ginger, nutmeg, cinnamon, and salt. Cut the margarine into very small pieces before incorporating them into the dry mix. Set the topping aside until ready to use.

Makes about 1 ½ cups

HONEYED YOGURT

½ cup 2% Greek yogurt   **2 tablespoons honey**   **Zest of ½ lemon**

In a small bowl whisk together the yogurt, honey, and lemon zest. Set aside in the refrigerator until ready to use.

Makes about ¾ cup.

EGG CUSTARD BRÛLÉE

One of the best ways we get ideas is by going through family recipe cards and being reminded of the things that were at the table when we were little. This egg custard is based on one of my grandmother Nannie's cards and is attributed to her friend Dot. Egg custard makes a wonderful pie, but here, brûléeing it and peppering it makes it a standout all on its own.

1 ½ cups whole milk

1 tablespoon unsalted butter

3 large eggs

½ cup plus 4 teaspoons cane sugar, divided

½ teaspoon vanilla extract

⅛ teaspoon nutmeg

Scant ⅛ teaspoon cracked black pepper

Pinch of sea salt flakes

Preheat your oven to 325 degrees F. Scald the milk by heating it on medium-high on the stovetop and stirring it constantly. Remove it from the heat as soon as it boils, and then add the butter. In a medium bowl beat the eggs and add ½ cup sugar. Add ¼ cup of hot milk to the egg mixture and whisk it well. Repeat a few times until the mixture is well mixed. Add vanilla and nutmeg.

Pour the custard into ramekins or shallow 5-inch brûlée dishes—the custard should be about 1 inch high. Put the filled dishes in a hot water bath so that the water comes halfway up the side of the vessel. Place in the oven and bake for 15 to 20 minutes or until the custard is just set in the middle. Cool for 30 minutes, and then remove them from the water bath.

Sprinkle each custard with 1 teaspoon of cane sugar and then broil them in the oven while watching them the entire time. It takes about 1 minute for the sugar to caramelize, and it happens quickly! Remove from the oven and top each custard with a pinch of pepper and a pinch of salt. Let them cool on the counter for 30 minutes. Put them in the fridge for at least an hour before serving.

Makes 4 servings.

DRINKS

Peanut Butter and Banana Smoothie 206

Spinach and Strawberry Green Smoothie 208

Sazerac Iced Tea 210

Easy Horchata 212

Juicer Bloody Marys 214

Melonade 217

Bourbon with Basil and Lemonade Granita 219

PEANUT BUTTER AND BANANA SMOOTHIE

This is one of our favorite drinks, and it is so simple to make. Plus, it's a great way to use up bananas that have gone a little dark. Just peel them, throw them into a food storage container, and place them in the freezer. They'll be ready next time you want this good-for-you frozen treat.

The ripe bananas have plenty of natural sweetness, and the peanuts are a great source of protein. The texture of the blended frozen bananas is a lot like a milkshake, so enjoy! It can be your breakfast in a cup or the perfect beverage to cool you down after a run when, like us, you're trying to stay on the cute side of chubby.

3 frozen medium bananas

¼ cup peanut butter (smooth or chunky)

1 ½ cups soy milk (or 2% milk)

½ cup 2% Greek yogurt

1 teaspoon honey

¼ teaspoon sea salt flakes

1 tablespoon chopped, roasted peanuts

Place the frozen bananas into a blender, along with the peanut butter, soy milk, yogurt, honey, and salt. Blend until smooth. Top each drink with a teaspoon of chopped peanuts.

Makes 2 smoothies.

SPINACH AND STRAWBERRY GREEN SMOOTHIE

Sure, green smoothies aren't all that attractive compared to the pleasing pastels of typical fruit smoothies, but just a few simple ingredients pack a healthy punch here. Fitting in an extra vegetable in the morning and getting a healthy energy boost are both good news. What's surprising is you'll barely taste the green in this smoothie!

2 cups loose-packed baby spinach

1 large frozen banana, peeled and roughly chopped

½ cup roughly chopped strawberries (about 5)

Juice of 3 oranges (about ¾ cup)

½ cup ice

In a blender add the spinach, banana, strawberries, orange juice, and ice. Blend on high until fully combined.

Makes 2 servings.

SAZERAC ICED TEA

A Sazerac cocktail is flush with so many complex notes: cinnamon, honey, herbs, mint, and a hint of dark tea. It's amazing, really. This nonalcoholic iced tea hits some of those same notes. It's quite delicious and festive, perfect for your first outdoor BBQ in the spring.

1 medium orange, sliced into rounds	¼ cup honey	6 cups hot water
¼ teaspoon Vietnamese cinnamon	2 sprigs fresh mint, divided	2 cups ice
	2 iced tea bags	

Place the sliced orange, cinnamon, honey, and one of the mint sprigs into a two-quart iced tea pitcher. Add the tea bags and hot water. Stir to incorporate the cinnamon and honey. Steep the tea for 3 minutes. Remove the tea bags and add ice. Add the reserved mint sprig to the pitcher. Serve poured over plenty of ice on a hot summer day.

Makes 4 servings.

EASY HORCHATA

This isn't the traditional way to make horchata, but it suits us just fine. Don't let the simplicity of this little treat fool you because it's delicious. Make this to go along with tacos or tamales—the sweet rice milk is the perfect foil for spicy food.

2 ½ cups vanilla rice milk

½ teaspoon ground cinnamon, plus a little extra for sprinkling

1 teaspoon light agave nectar

Ice (to fill two tall drinking glasses)

Place the milk, cinnamon, and agave nectar into a cocktail shaker, and shake vigorously for about 30 seconds. You want it to get a little foam on top. Pour the mixture over ice and sprinkle the top of each drink with a pinch of cinnamon.

Makes 2 servings.

JUICER BLOODY MARYS

Once we purchased a juicer, we experimented for a while and came up with some healthy, potent juices like apple-carrot-spinach and clementine-ginger. It wasn't long before we were looking for a more sinister use for the juice: a juicer bloody Mary. It is the perfect companion for the black-eyed peas, greens, and cornbread at a New Year's Day party. Because everything is fresh, our version of this brunch beverage tastes light and clean compared to the thick, preservative-heavy mixes. Try this recipe for yourself—with or without the vodka.

Special equipment: a juicer

8 to 10 large Roma tomatoes

1 stalk celery (use small ribs and leaves as garnish)

1 large cucumber

1 green bell pepper

1 jalapeño (pull out the seeds and ribs if you like it mild)

2 medium carrots

1 clove garlic

2 limes

2 teaspoons vegetarian Worcestershire sauce

1 tablespoon tomato paste

½ teaspoon sea salt flakes

Cracked black pepper (to taste)

10 ounces vodka (optional)

8 pieces of pickled okra (or pickled beans) (to garnish)

8 small inner celery ribs with tops (to garnish)

Rinse the vegetables and limes. (There's no need to peel if you have a powerful juicer.) Juice the tomatoes, celery, cucumber, bell pepper, jalapeño, carrots, garlic, and limes. Pour the juices into a large pitcher. Add the Worcestershire sauce, tomato paste, salt, and pepper, and stir. Pour over ice to serve. Add vodka if you like and garnish with pickled okra and celery tops.

Makes 8 servings.

MELONADE

This whimsical drink takes a little time to make, but what could be better on a really hot day than a glass of melonade? It's quite refreshing, in addition to looking pretty, so the work really is worth it.

1 medium cantaloupe	Juice of 1 lime	⅛ teaspoon sea salt flakes
1 medium honeydew melon	Juice of 4 lemons	1 cup water
1 watermelon (personal size)	⅓ cup light agave syrup	

Wash the melons and cut them in half using a large knife. Remove any seeds by scraping them out with a spoon. Discard the seeds. Next, use a melon baller to scoop out round spheres of melon; the flesh from the top of the half will be the firmest and easiest to scoop, so be sure to dig deeply into it and then twist. Scoop as many as you can from one half of each melon. Place the melon balls in the freezer.

Cut the rest of the flesh from the remaining halves of the melons so that you have about 1 cup of each. Place this pulp in the food processor and blend until smooth. Use a mesh strainer to strain the melon juice into a bowl; use a silicone spatula to press out all the juice. To the strained melon juice, add the juice from the lime and lemons and the agave. Whisk together, and then add salt and water before whisking again. Place the semi-frozen melon balls in a pitcher and add the juice and ice. Stir and serve over ice.

Makes 4 servings.

BOURBON WITH BASIL AND LEMONADE GRANITA

When your herb garden is full of basil and you've had it up to here with pesto, don't let all that summery goodness go to waste! May we suggest basil and lemonade granita?

This is the perfect after-dinner drink for the waning days of summer—especially if you're looking to make the last painful stretch of Southern heat (somewhat) bearable. This is one to sip slowly on the front porch as the summer sun sets.

2 cups loose-packed
fresh basil leaves

2 cups water

½ cup cane sugar

¼ cup honey

Juice of 6 lemons
(about 1 cup)

7 ½ ounces bourbon
(optional)

Add the basil leaves, water, sugar, and honey to a saucepan, bring to a boil, and cook for 5 minutes. Allow the mixture to cool. Strain out the leaves and add the lemon juice. Place the mixture in a pan or a wide-mouth bowl and freeze. Be sure to scrape the surface with a fork every hour until the mixture is frozen solid. This should take about 3 hours.

To serve, use a medium ice-cream scoop and put a full scoop of the frozen basil mixture in each glass. Then add 1 ¼ ounces of your favorite bourbon.

Makes 6 servings.

BASIC RECIPES

3-2-1 Buttermilk Drop Biscuits (with Cheddar and Buttermilk variations) 222

Simple Smoky Salsa 223

Beer Pizza Crust 224

Memphis BBQ Dry Rub 225

Chipotle BBQ Sauce 226

Basic Piecrust Dough 227

No-Bones-About-It Vegetarian Broth 228

Vegetable-Packed Tomato Sauce 229

Mushroom Meat 230

The Chubby Vegetarian Quick-Smoking Method 231

Sea Salt Granola 232

Charred Corn and Avocado Salsa 233

3-2-1 BUTTERMILK DROP BISCUITS (WITH CHEDDAR AND BUTTERMILK VARIATIONS)

3 tablespoons baking powder

2 cups all-purpose flour

½ teaspoon iodized salt

¼ cup organic vegetable shortening or unsalted butter

1 cup milk

Preheat your oven to 425 degrees F. Whisk the baking powder, all-purpose flour, and salt in a large bowl. Using your fingers, cut in the shortening or butter until pieces are no larger than a pea.

Make a well in the center of the flour mixture. Add the buttermilk. Using a rubber spatula, fold the milk into the dry ingredients. Use as few strokes as possible because the less you stir the dough, the more tender your biscuits will be.

Use a medium spring-action ice-cream scoop to scoop up a ¼-cup portion of dough and drop it onto a parchment-lined baking sheet. Repeat until all of the dough has been used. Be sure to leave an inch or so between each biscuit, but don't be too particular about their shape—drop biscuits are supposed to be rustic. Bake for 15 minutes or until the craggy edges are brown and crispy.

Makes 10 to 12 biscuits.

Variations: To make Cheddar 3-2-1 Drop Biscuits, add one cup of shredded sharp Cheddar or smoked Cheddar to the dry ingredients.

To make Buttermilk 3-2-1 Drop Biscuits, substitute 1 ¼ cups buttermilk for the whole milk.

Note: These biscuits are best right out of the oven, but they can be cooked, frozen, and reheated if necessary. To reheat, place frozen biscuits on a parchment-lined baking sheet, brush the tops with melted butter, and place into a 350° F. oven until the tops are nicely browned. The result is a crispier, slightly richer biscuit that is still moist and tender inside.

SIMPLE SMOKY SALSA

Use this salsa recipe to add flavor to eggs, tamales, or just place it near a bowl of corn chips. You'll never want to buy salsa from a jar again.

2 medium tomatoes

1 medium jalapeño pepper, stem removed

2 cloves unpeeled garlic

Juice from 1 lime

⅛ teaspoon cane sugar

Sea salt flakes and cracked pepper to taste

In a medium cast-iron skillet over high heat, burn the outside of the tomatoes, jalapeño, and the garlic (still in its papery skin). Do this by turning the tomatoes, jalapeño, and garlic every 3 to 4 minutes using kitchen tongs. Once all sides are blackened, remove and set aside in a bowl to cool. Using a paring knife, core the tomatoes and place in the work bowl of your food processor. Squeeze the head of garlic from the root end, and the cloves should pop right out. Add them to the food processor along with the jalapeño, lime juice, sugar, and salt and pepper to taste. Pulse the food processor until all ingredients are well incorporated, but still chunky.

Makes about 1 ½ cups.

BEER PIZZA CRUST

Pizza is the great equalizer when one's considering what to feed a mixed group of vegetarians and non-vegetarians. It's rare that anyone is ever disappointed in a pizza no matter what's on top, so serving it to a crowd is usually a no-brainer. Use this recipe to make our BBQ Tofu Pizza or our Peach and Tarragon Pesto Pizza.

Sometimes we like to par-cook my homemade pizza crust. It allows for less time in the kitchen when friends and family are over, and it ensures a good product. All you do is throw the dough, slide it onto the stone, and cook it for just a few minutes. When it's time to eat, top your par-cooked crusts with sauce and cheese, and slide 'em into the oven to crisp up.

9 to 12 ounces beer	1 ½ cups all-purpose flour	1 teaspoon honey
1 ½ cups bread flour	½ teaspoon iodized sea salt	1 teaspoon Rapid-Rise yeast

Pour the beer into a microwave-safe glass and heat for 1 minute. Place the bread flour and all-purpose flour, salt, and honey into a stand mixer, turn it on low, and add the yeast. Slowly add the beer until all the dry flour has been incorporated. You will need between 8 and 10 ounces of beer—there will be beer left over. Mix for 5 minutes until the dough looks smooth.

Divide the dough in half. Roll each piece into a ball; place each in its own airtight container with plenty of space for the dough to rise. Set the containers out on the countertop. Leave the dough alone for 1 hour. In the meantime place a pizza stone in the oven and preheat to 500 degrees F.

Turn the dough ball out onto a lightly floured pizza peel. Begin to dimple the dough using three fingers. The middle of the dough should look like the surface of a golf ball. Leave ½ inch on the outside undisturbed—this will become the crust. Turn the dough over and repeat the process. Pick up the dough, and let it stretch over your fists until it is about 12 inches in diameter, or toss it in the air like a pro—your call. Make sure you have enough flour on the peel so that the pizza can slide around and into the oven. You may use a piece of parchment paper instead of flour, which is easier for a beginner. Place the raw crust on a sheet of parchment paper. Add any topping that you like at this point. Using the pizza peel, slide the raw pizza onto the hot stone, and let it cook for 7 minutes. Remove the pizza once the top starts bubbling and it begins to brown around the edges. Cut and serve.

Makes two 12-inch pizzas crusts.

MEMPHIS BBQ DRY RUB

Making a dry rub is easy—and there's no real rhyme or reason to it. We've been told stories of people emptying the contents of their spice cabinet into a large jar to create their "signature" rub. Our own spicy dry rub usually contains the key ingredients in equal measure. If you try it once, you may never BBQ anything without a dry rub again.

1 teaspoon chipotle powder

1 teaspoon sweet paprika

1 teaspoon smoked paprika

1 teaspoon granulated garlic

1 teaspoon iodized sea salt

1 teaspoon cumin

1 teaspoon cinnamon

1 teaspoon ground ginger

1 teaspoon cracked black pepper

1 teaspoon light brown sugar

1 teaspoon dried oregano

Mix spices together in a small bowl. Save any extra in a food storage container for up to a year.

Makes ¼ cup.

CHIPOTLE BBQ SAUCE

This is a bold, spicy, smoky BBQ sauce when you taste it on its own, but it evens out nicely when applied to tofu or mushrooms.

1 tablespoon unsalted butter

2 cups chopped onion (about 1 medium)

¼ cup chopped garlic (about 6 medium cloves)

½ teaspoon garlic powder

½ teaspoon dried thyme

¼ teaspoon cracked black pepper

2 tablespoons Tennessee whiskey

½ cup firmly packed light brown sugar

¼ cup apple cider vinegar

3 to 4 ounces chipotle peppers from a can (about ½ can)

½ cup water

1 (24-ounce) bottle of organic ketchup

1 tablespoon soy sauce

1 tablespoon vegetarian Worcestershire

1 tablespoon mustard

1 teaspoon liquid smoke

In a medium saucepan over medium-high heat, melt the butter and start to sweat the onion and garlic. Use a wooden spoon to keep the mixture moving so as not to burn the garlic. Once the onion is translucent, add the garlic powder, thyme, and black pepper. Deglaze the pan with the whiskey, and cook until all liquid has evaporated. Reduce the heat to medium-low. Add the brown sugar, vinegar, chipotle peppers, water, ketchup, soy sauce, Worcestershire, mustard, and liquid smoke. Simmer uncovered for an hour, and stir occasionally to keep the sauce from scorching.

You need only 1 cup of sauce for the BBQ Tofu, but this sauce freezes well.

Makes 6 cups.

BASIC PIECRUST DOUGH

This piecrust dough is the basis for many of our recipes including hand pies, dessert pies, pot pie, and galettes. It is so easy to make your own that there's no need to buy premade piecrust.

1 ½ cups all-purpose flour

⅓ cup organic vegetable shortening

½ teaspoon iodized sea salt

About ⅓ cup ice water

Place the flour, shortening, and salt into the food processor. Turn it on and allow it to run for a few seconds so the shortening becomes incorporated into the flour. Add the water 1 teaspoon at a time until the dough comes together by forming itself into a ball and rolling around the inside of the work bowl. Wrap the dough in plastic wrap, and place it in the fridge to rest for 20 minutes.

Makes 2 piecrusts.

NO-BONES-ABOUT-IT VEGETARIAN BROTH

Why make your own vegetarian broth? Why not? It's fresh, it's better than anything in a can or a carton, and really, it's not that hard. The process is simple: Begin by using a food processor to allow the maximum amount of flavor to be extracted from the vegetables in a minimum amount of time. Then boil. Strain. Simmer. Done.

Soups taste so much better this way. This broth is great in tomato sauce, curries, grits, and beans as well. You can make a big batch of this broth, use some, and freeze the remainder until you need it.

2 tablespoons olive oil

1 large onion, roughly chopped

4 medium carrots, roughly chopped

4 ribs celery (with leaves)

2 green bell peppers

2 medium Roma tomatoes

1 bulb of garlic, unpeeled (remove the root end)

2 cups loose-packed fresh flat-leaf parsley

7 sprigs fresh thyme

2 bay leaves

2 tablespoons red miso

1 ½ teaspoons whole black peppercorns

4 quarts water

1 lemon, halved

Iodized sea salt (to taste)

Heat the olive oil on medium-high heat, and then sauté the chopped onion in the oil until it's translucent and starting to brown around the edges. In batches, process the onions, carrots, celery, bell peppers, tomatoes, and garlic in the food processor. Put all the processed vegetables and garlic into a large soup pot, and add the parsley, thyme, bay leaves, miso, and peppercorns. Add the 4 quarts of water. Squeeze the lemon halves into the pot and then drop them right in with the other ingredients. Bring it all to a boil, then simmer for 20 minutes.

Let cool, and then strain. Discard all but the liquid and return the liquid to the soup pot. Cook on medium-high heat until reduced by half. This could take up to 30 minutes. Season with salt to taste.

Makes 2 quarts.

TIP: A variation on this is to add 12 ounces roasted or 4 ounces dried mushrooms; the mushrooms will make the broth more "beefy" and savory.

VEGETABLE-PACKED TOMATO SAUCE

Save the odds and ends from your cooking for the month—mushrooms, bell peppers, eggplant, tomatoes, spinach, greens, pesto, pine nuts, red wine, olives, and so on—and freeze them for the base of this amazing tomato sauce.

Up to 8 cups vegetable trimmings (from the freezer)

1/4 cup olive oil, divided

2 medium carrots, chopped

2 ribs celery, chopped

1 large white onion, chopped

2 tablespoons Italian seasoning

1/2 cup white wine (like Pinot Grigio)

2 tablespoons balsamic vinegar

1 tablespoon cane sugar

5 cups diced tomatoes

1 tube tomato paste

1 head of garlic, peeled (8 to 12 cloves)

Iodized sea salt and cracked black pepper (to taste)

Preheat your oven to 425 degrees F. Place the frozen vegetable trimmings (stems and cores removed) on a 17 x 12-inch rimmed baking sheet. Drizzle with 1/8 cup olive oil. Cook for 30 to 45 minutes or until the vegetables begin to brown on top. Remove and set aside.

Put remaining 1/8 cup olive oil into a large stockpot on medium heat, and place the chopped carrots, celery, and onions in the pot. Sweat the vegetables until the onions are translucent. Add the Italian seasoning, white wine, vinegar, and sugar, and reduce for 5 minutes or until most of the liquid has evaporated. Add the diced tomatoes and tomato paste, and bring to a simmer. Add the roasted vegetables. Using an immersion blender, blend the sauce until smooth. Add water or stock to adjust the thickness of the sauce. Add sea salt and cracked black pepper to taste. Cover and cook the sauce for 1 hour.

Makes about 5 cups.

MUSHROOM MEAT

We used to rely on meat substitutes to give our meals that old, familiar texture and flavor that we grew up with as the center of our 1980s meat-and-three dinners. As we began to shy away from more processed foods, we were looking for a way to get that same familiar result from our own kitchen. The solution was to take two things we already love, mushrooms and eggplant, and turn them into a multipurpose "meat." It's so simple and requires little hands-on time. Make this in large batches, freeze what you don't use, and defrost it to add to tacos or burritos, to fill tamales, or to cobble together a homemade veggie burger.

3 cups finely chopped portobello mushrooms (about 3 medium, stems included)

3 cups finely chopped eggplant, peeled (about 1 medium)

2 cups finely chopped white onion (about 1 medium)

2 vegetarian bouillon cubes

¼ cup olive oil

2 tablespoons balsamic vinegar

1 teaspoon garlic powder

⅛ teaspoon cracked black pepper

Preheat your oven to 350 degrees F. Add the roughly chopped mushrooms, stems and all, to your food processor and pulse three times or until finely chopped. The pieces should be about the size of a black-eyed pea. (Do not overwork the mushrooms or they will turn into a paste.) Place the processed mushrooms onto a large, parchment-lined, 17 x 12-inch rimmed baking sheet. Pulse the roughly chopped eggplant in the food processor in the same manner. Place the eggplant onto the sheet pan with the mushrooms. Repeat this process with the onion.

Crumble the bouillon cubes into the pile of processed vegetables. Drizzle the mound of mushrooms, eggplant, and onion with the olive oil and vinegar. Using your hands, toss it all together. Spread the mixture evenly over the sheet pan. Sprinkle with the garlic powder and pepper. Bake for a total of 20 minutes. Remove the mixture and allow it to cool in the pan.

Makes 4 cups.

NOTE: *Some eggplants will contain more water than others. If there is excess moisture in the bottom of the pan, drain it off using a colander. Reserve the flavorful liquid to add to soups or stews.*

VARIATIONS: *For an Italian variation, add fresh herbs from the garden. To make a Mexican version, add cumin to the mix, along with a palmful of ancho chili powder and chipotle pepper. The possibilities are endless. Substitute Mushroom Meat in any recipe that calls for ground beef.*

THE CHUBBY VEGETARIAN QUICK-SMOKING METHOD

Many grill-top or stove-top smokers are available these days. You can find them online or at almost any specialty kitchen store. I made my own using a 12 x 9-inch stainless steel pan with a shallow, perforated basket and a tight-fitting lid. You could also use an old stock pot with a lid and an old footed colander that will fit down inside the pot. (Just remember, the lid has to fit tightly to keep the smoke in, and anything you use has to be dedicated to smoking—it will be completely ruined for any other purpose.) The large pan has to be at least 1 inch deeper than the perforated pan so there's room for the wood chips. You'll also need an outdoor gas grill and some wood chips, which are available in most grocery stores—especially during the summer months.

The following instructions work for smoking any non-meltable foods like mushrooms, dates, grapes, sun-dried tomatoes, potatoes, sea salt, or tofu. Do not try this method with a cheese that will melt because it will melt unattractively. That said, this is a wonderful and simple way to impart a ton of flavor into some very unexpected ingredients.

1. Soak a handful of hickory wood chips and two handfuls of applewood chips in water for about 20 minutes. This is the best mix of pungent hickory and fruity applewood smoke. But if you like a less intense smoke flavor, try all-fruit woods, like apple or cherry.
2. Drain the chips and set them in the bottom of your smoker pan. Turn your grill on high. Do not do this inside as it produces a lot of smoke! Place the smoker pan directly over the flame of your outdoor gas grill (the side burner works best for this). After 8 minutes, you will notice a lot of smoke coming from the chips; this is a good thing!
3. Lay your mushrooms, dates, tomatoes, garlic, or anything else you want to taste smoky in a single layer in the smoker basket, and place over the smoking wood chips.
4. Cover with a tight-fitting lid. Smoke for 5 minutes. It doesn't take long for vegetables to soak up the smoky flavor. Remove whatever you just smoked from the basket and allow it all to cool. Keep the smoked items in an airtight container for up to a week.

SEA SALT GRANOLA

This salty, crunchy, sweet-but-bordering-on-savory granola never lasts very long around our house. Store-bought granola doesn't even come close to it, and people love receiving it as a gift. It begs to be used on a sophisticated salad, but you also should try it with yogurt and fruit for breakfast or just on its own as a quick, portable snack. Sometimes we add chocolate chunks to it when it's still warm since the only thing better than granola is chocolate-covered granola.

¼ cup light brown sugar

¼ cup brown rice syrup*

⅓ cup canola oil

2 teaspoons vanilla extract

1 tablespoon sea salt flakes

2 cups rolled oats

⅓ cup sliced almonds, raw and unsalted

⅓ cup pecans, raw and unsalted

⅓ cup pumpkin seeds, raw and unsalted

Preheat your oven to 350 degrees F. Whisk the sugar, syrup, oil, vanilla, and salt. Add the oats, almonds, pecans, and pumpkin seeds, and combine. Spread it all out on a baking sheet. Bake for 10 minutes, stir it up, and then bake it for 10 more minutes. Let it cool on a parchment-lined plate. It'll keep for up to a week in a sealed container.

Makes 3 ½ cups.

*Brown rice syrup is a key ingredient here, so make the effort to find it. It is available at natural foods stores.

CHARRED CORN AND AVOCADO SALSA

2 ears corn

2 cups diced avocado
(about 2 medium)

Juice from 1 lime

2 tablespoons minced
fresh cilantro

2 green onions, thinly sliced

1 teaspoon olive oil

Sea salt flakes and cracked
black pepper (to taste)

Over a high flame on your outdoor grill, char the ears of corn until lightly blackened, about 4 minutes per side. Using a sharp knife and plenty of caution, cut the corn away from the cob. In a medium bowl combine the corn, avocado, lime juice, cilantro, green onion, and olive oil. Add sea salt and cracked black pepper to taste.

Makes 2 ½ cups.

THANK YOU SO MUCH, Y'ALL

This book is here due to your help, support, and advice.

For those we miss: LF Beard, UM and Juanita Gibbs, Suzanne Burks, Charlene and Odell Burks, and Wilma Gibbs.

And for those who are always so supportive:

Steve and Blandy Lawrence and Concord Farms
Mary Beard
Graham Burks, Sr. and Virginia Maier
Ray Baum and Diane Lawrence
Moishe, Lindsey, and Amelia Lettvin
Hunter Burks
Graham Burks, Jr., Bianca Burks, Graham Burks III, and Fox Christian Burks
Marshall, Jean Marie, Becca, and Neely Burks
The Beard, Campbell, and Stringer families
The Gibbs and the Sellers families
The Matlock and Mead families
Aaron, Renee, Rocco, and Calliope Brame
Kelly Robinson and Michael Hughes
Aaron, Jaimee, Catherine, and Charlotte Cooley
John Currence of City Grocery Restaurant Group
Kelly English of Restaurant Iris
Jennifer Chandler
Melissa Petersen of *Edible Memphis*
Susan Ellis of Contemporary Media
Pamela Denney of *Memphis Magazine*
Bianca Phillips of Vegan Crunk
Mary Helen Randall
Jill and Keith Forrester of Whitton Farms and the Trolley Stop
Van Cheeseman of Flora at Bluebird Farms
Marshall Boswell
Natalie Parker-Lawrence
Emily Lux and Whole Foods Market
Heather Skelton of Thomas Nelson
Warren Oster and Stacey Greenberg
Max Maloney and Marlinee Clark

Gary Backus and Margot McNeeley of Project Green Fork
Andrew Adams and Wally Joe of Acre and The Brushmark
Andria Lisle of the Brooks Museum
Andrew Holiday of Harvest Creative
Craig and Elizabeth Blondis
J.C. and Danielle Youngblood
John and Wendy Rylee
Cameron and Amy Mann
David and Joann Bell
Andrew Ticer and Michael Hudman of Andrew Michael Italian Kitchen
Felicia Willett of Felicia Suzanne's
Ryan Trimm of Sweet Grass
Jason Quinn of The Playground
Robert and Tara Gordon
Glenda Hastings and Rusty Prudhomme of Napa Café
Krishna R. Chattu of Mayuri Indian Cuisine
Chris Hawkins
Ben Vaughn
Jody Moyt of Owen Brennan's
Rick Saviori
Jason Doty
Joe Morris
Nick Rogers
John T. Edge of The Southern Foodways Alliance
Jesse Kimball of The Memphis Tap Room
Our friends at *The Memphis Flyer*, *Memphis Magazine*, Rhodes College, and
   Hutchison School

All of our recipe testers, including the following shining stars: Louisa, Trevor, Angie,
Kate, Kristy, Hannah, Heather, Margot, Shauna, Bianca, Jason B., Julie B., Allison, Jen,
Julie T., Aaron, Reneé, Tiffany, Teresa, An, Becca G., Melissa B., Karen, Wendy R., Leslie P.,
Jamiee, Susie, Stephanie, Chip, Chris, Taylor, Rachel C., Lindsey, Kerri, Danielle, Francesca,
Graham Sr., Wendy, Jennifer, Hannah, Sarah, CWK, April, Michael, Diane, Ray, Becky,
Jason D., Shannon, Antigone, Andrew O., Tara, Lesley L., Huda, and Merry Beth

ABOUT THE AUTHORS

Justin Fox Burks and Amy Lawrence, a husband-and-wife team, are the authors of *The Southern Vegetarian Cookbook*. A lifelong vegetarian, Justin's career as a photographer allows him access to the secrets of some of the South's greatest kitchens, where he picks up tips and tricks from talented chefs. Justin's food photography has appeared in *Food & Wine*, *Garden & Gun*, *Mojo*, *Memphis Magazine*, and the *London Independent*; in addition, he writes for *Edible Memphis* and the *Memphis Flyer*.

Amy Lawrence studied the dishes and techniques of restaurant chefs as a food writer; she was the Dining Out column restaurant critic for *Memphis Magazine* from 2009 to 2011 and often writes about home cooking for *Edible Memphis* and the *Memphis Flyer*. She teaches English at Hutchison School.

Justin and Amy's blog, The Chubby Vegetarian, was awarded Blog of Note in 2010, and in 2011, caught the attention of producers and Tyler Florence of the Food Network's *The Great Food Truck Race*. As a result, Justin was a guest judge on the show's vegetarian challenge in Memphis, and the blog was highlighted on the show.

Justin and Amy have developed vegetarian dinners and events at some of the greatest restaurants in the heart of BBQ land and are proud to be helping people love their vegetables. Married for nine years, they continue to cook and create in Memphis, Tennessee.

INDEX

3-2-1 Buttermilk Drop Biscuits (with Cheddar and
 Buttermilk variations), 222
20-Minute Tamales, 126–127

acorn squash, Chanterelle and Apricot Stuffed
 Acorn Squash with Miracle Mushroom Gravy,
 136
Adams, Andrew, 122
agave nectar, Easy Horchata, 212
agave syrup, Melonade, 217
almond butter, xviii
almonds, xviii
 Sea Salt Granola, 232
 Tofu Almondine in a White Wine-Butter
 Sauce, 157–158
 Vegetarian Country Captain, 119
Andouille eggplant, 174
appetizers
 BBQ Tofu Nachos with Chipotle Pinto Beans
 and Guacamole, 37–38
 Deviled Egg and Olive, 58
 Green Pea Hummus, 39
 Hoppin' John Black-Eyed Pea Butter, 56
 Lime Truck's Corn Cake with BBQ Slaw, 28–29
 Mini Potato and Buttermilk Pancakes with
 Beluga Lentils and Crème Fraîche, 46–47
 Natchitoches Umami Pies with Yogurt
 Chimichurri, 31–32
 Okra Fritters with Creole Mustard Sauce, 41
 Oyster Mushroom Rockefeller, 43–44
 Sambal Pepper Jelly and Savory Cheddar-
 Pecan Cookies, 33–34
 Smoked Dates Stuffed with Goat Cheese and
 Pecans, 53
 Southern-Style Cheese Dip, 54
 Tofu and Truffle "Pork" Rinds, 49
 Zucchini Fries, 50
apple cider vinegar, xx
apples
 Apple, Cheddar, and Thyme Galette, 14
 Triple-Ginger Apple Crisp, 200
 Vegetarian Country Captain, 119
apricots, Chanterelle and Apricot Stuffed Acorn
 Squash with Miracle Mushroom Gravy, 136

artichokes
 Artichoke Hearts and Succotash over Smoked
 Cheddar Grits, 143–144
 preparing, 115
 Vegetarian Frogmore Stew, 114
 Vegetarian "Midnight Snack" Inspired by
 Restaurant Iris, 77
arugula, Crispy Eggplant Sandwiches and Roasted
 Garlic and Ricotta Spread, 79
avocados
 Charred Corn and Avocado Salsa, 233
 No-Fuss Guacamole, 38
 Tacos with Spicy, Smoky Lentils, 125
 Watermelon and Tomato Gazpacho, 106

baking sheets, xvi
balsamic vinaigrette, 70
balsamic vinegar, xx
 balsamic reduction, 160
bananas
 Mascarpone Banana Pudding, 192
 Peanut Butter and Banana Smoothie, 206
 Spinach and Strawberry Green Smoothie, 208
 Super-Moist Banana Muffins, 20
Basic Piecrust Dough
 Bourbon Pecan Tart, 188
 Nannie's Blueberry Pie, 185
 Vegetarian "Chicken" Pot Pie, 134
 Zucchini and Tomato Galette, 133
Basil Compound Butter, 197
basil leaves
 Bourbon with Basil and Lemonade Granita, 219
 Caprese Salad in a Jar, 70
BBQ dry rub, Memphis BBQ Dry Rub, 225
BBQ Portobello Mushroom Sandwich with
 Smoked Gouda, 91
BBQ sauce, Chipotle BBQ Sauce, 226
BBQ Slaw, Corn Cake with, 28–29
BBQ Tofu Nachos with Chipotle Pinto Beans and
 Guacamole, 37–38
BBQ Tofu Pizza, 140
bean curd sheets, Tofu and Truffle "Pork" Rinds, 49
beans, xviii. *See also* black beans
 Chipotle Pinto Beans, 38

garbanzo
    garbanzo bean flour, xviii
    Vegetarian Country Captain, 119
red
    Chubby Vegetarian Gumbo, 111
    Vegetarian Red Beans and Rice with
        Andouille Eggplant, 170
Beer Pizza Crust, 224
    for BBQ Tofu Pizza, 140
    for Peach and Tarragon Pesto Pizza, 131
beets, Roast Beet Salad with Sea Salt Granola
    and Honey-Tarragon Dressing, 67
Belgian waffles, Vegetarian "Chicken" and
    Waffles, 122
bell peppers
    Juicer Bloody Marys, 214
    Lemon Zest and Thyme Pimento Cheese, 84
    Ratatouille Napoleon, 159–160
    Saffron Egg Drop Soup, 105
    Smoky Grilled Vegetable Quesadillas, 99
    succotash, 143–144
    Vegan Peanut Chili with Charred Corn and
        Avocado Salsa, 162
    Vegan Sloppy Joes, 97
    Vegetarian "Chicken" Pot Pie, 134
    Vegetarian Meatloaf with Garlic Mashed
        Potatoes, 166–168
    Vegetarian Red Beans and Rice with Andouille
        Eggplant, 170
    Watermelon and Tomato Gazpacho, 106
beluga lentils, Mini Potato and Buttermilk
    Pancakes with Beluga Lentils and Crème
    Fraîche, 46–47
bench scraper, xvi
biscuits, 3-2-1 Buttermilk Drop Biscuits (with
    Cheddar and Buttermilk variations), 222
black beans
    Natchitoches Umami Pies with Yogurt
        Chimichurri, 31
    seasoned, 12
black-eyed peas, Hoppin' John Black-Eyed Pea
    Butter, 56
black truffle oil, xvii
blender, xv
Bloody Marys, Juicer, 214
blue cheese, Fried Chickpea Sandwich with Blue
    Cheese and Tomato, 86
blueberries, Nannie's Blueberry Pie, 185
bocconcini, Caprese Salad in a Jar, 70

boeuf bourguignon, vegetarian, 163–164
boudin sausage, vegetarian, 151
bouillon cubes, xxi
Bourbon Pecan Tart, 188
Bourbon with Basil and Lemonade Granita, 219
Bragg Liquid Aminos, xix
bran muffins, Vegan Bran Muffins, 24
bread, brioche, 77
bread crumbs, xviii
    Vegetarian Meatballs, 154
breakfast and brunch
    Apple, Cheddar, and Thyme Galette, 14
    French Toast Pancake, 18
    Miracle Mushroom Gravy, 8
    Simple Smoky Migas Bowl, 12
    Smoked Sun-Dried Tomato Tortilla with
        Herbed Aioli, 10
    Southern Benedict with Wilted Spinach and
        Espresso Redeye Gravy, 5–6
    Super-Moist Banana Muffins, 20
    Sweet Potato Grits with Maple Mushrooms
        and a Fried Egg, 3–4
    Sweet Potato Pancakes with Peaches and
        Pecans, 17
    Toasted Coconut Muffins, 22
    Vegan Bran Muffins, 24
brioche bread, Vegetarian "Midnight Snack"
    Inspired by Restaurant Iris, 77
broth, No-Bones-About-It Vegetarian Broth, 228
brown rice, xviii
    Brown Rice and Brown Butter Crispies, 183
brown rice syrup, 188
    Sea Salt Granola, 232
brown sugar, xix
brûlée, egg custard, 202
brussels sprouts, Warm Brussels Sprout Salad with
    Smoked Feta and Candied Pecans, 68
burgers, Simple and Easy Porcini Mushroom
    Veggie Burgers, 94
butter, xvii
    Basil Compound Butter, 197
buttermilk pancakes, 46
buttermilk, Southern-Style Cheese Dip, 54
Butternut Squash Rotini Mac and Cheese, 175

cabbage
    BBQ Slaw, 29
    BBQ Tofu Pizza, 140
    Tacos with Spicy, Smoky Lentils, 125

cake, Nannie's Pound Cake, 186
canola oil, xvii
cantaloupe, Melonade, 217
Caprese Salad in a Jar, 70
Carolina Gold rice, xviii
carrots, xxi
    Dirty Fried Rice, 148
    Juicer Bloody Marys, 214
    Porcini and Portobello Mushroom
        Bourguignon over Smashed Potatoes,
        163–164
    porcini mushroom broth, 164
    Vegan Sloppy Joes, 97
    Vegetable-Packed Tomato Sauce, 229
    Vegetarian "Chicken" Pot Pie, 134
    Vegetarian Meatloaf with Garlic Mashed
        Potatoes, 166–168
    Vegetarian Roasted Red Pepper and Olive
        Muffuletta, 92
cauliflower
    Curried Cauliflower Soup, 102
    garlic mashed potatoes, 167
    Vegetarian Roasted Red Pepper and Olive
        Muffuletta, 92
celery, xxi
    Chubby Vegetarian Gumbo, 111
    Dirty Fried Rice, 148
    Juicer Bloody Marys, 214
    Vegan Sloppy Joes, 97
    Vegetable-Packed Tomato Sauce, 229
    Vegetarian Boudin Sausage, 151
    Vegetarian "Chicken" Pot Pie, 134
    Vegetarian Meatloaf with Garlic Mashed
        Potatoes, 166–168
    Vegetarian Red Beans and Rice with Andouille
        Eggplant, 170
champagne vinegar, xx
Chanterelle and Apricot Stuffed Acorn Squash
  with Miracle Mushroom Gravy, 136
Charred Corn and Avocado Salsa, 162, 233
cheddar cheese
    3-2-1 Buttermilk Drop Biscuits (with Cheddar
        and Buttermilk variations), 222
    Apple, Cheddar, and Thyme Galette, 14
    BBQ Tofu Nachos with Chipotle Pinto Beans
        and Guacamole, 37
    Lemon Zest and Thyme Pimento Cheese, 84
    Simple and Easy Porcini Mushroom Veggie
        Burgers, 94

Smoked Cheddar Jalapeño Cornbread, 153
Southern-Style Cheese Dip, 54
Tacos with Spicy, Smoky Lentils, 125
Triple Tomato Soup with Toasted White
    Cheddar Crouton, 100
cheddar grits, Artichoke Hearts and Succotash
  over Smoked Cheddar Grits, 143
Cheddar Jalapeño Cornbread, use in salad, 62
Cheddar-Pecan Cookies, 33–34
cheese
    blue, Fried Chickpea Sandwich with Blue
        Cheese and Tomato, 86
    cheddar
        3-2-1 Buttermilk Drop Biscuits (with
            Cheddar and Buttermilk variations), 222
        Apple, Cheddar, and Thyme Galette, 14
        BBQ Tofu Nachos with Chipotle Pinto
            Beans and Guacamole, 37
        Butternut Squash Rotini Mac and
            Cheese, 175
        Lemon Zest and Thyme Pimento
            Cheese, 84
        Simple and Easy Porcini Mushroom Veggie
            Burgers, 94
        Smoked Cheddar Jalapeño
            Cornbread, 153
        Southern-Style Cheese Dip, 54
        Tacos with Spicy, Smoky Lentils, 125
        Triple Tomato Soup with Toasted White
            Cheddar Crouton, 100
    Cotija, Mexican Corn Chowder, 108
    goat
        Butternut Squash Rotini Mac and
            Cheese, 175
        Fried Green Tomato Po' Boy, 88
        Grilled Watermelon and Tomato Salad with
            Honey-Lime Vinaigrette, 61
        Lemon Zest and Thyme Pimento
            Cheese, 84
        mushroom stuffing, 128–129
        Peach and Tarragon Pesto Pizza, 131
        Roast Beet Salad with Sea Salt Granola and
            Honey-Tarragon Dressing, 67
        Simple Smoke Migas Bowl, 12
        Smoked Dates Stuffed with Goat Cheese
            and Pecans, 53
    manchego
        Peach and Tarragon Pesto Pizza, 131
        Saffron Egg Drop Soup, 105

Smoked Sun-Dried Tomato Tortilla with
 Herbed Aioli, 10
mascarpone cheese, Mascarpone Banana
 Pudding, 192
Neufchâtel cheese, Nannie's Pound Cake, 186
Oaxaca
 Smoky Grilled Vegetable Quesadillas, 99
 Southern-Style Cheese Dip, 54
parmesan
 Crispy Eggplant Sandwiches and Roasted
  Garlic and Ricotta Spread, 79
 Oyster Mushroom Rockefeller, 43
 Roasted Garlic and Ricotta Spread, 80
 Southern Caesar Salad with Cornbread
  Croutons, 62
 Vegetarian Meatballs, 154
 Zucchini and Tomato Galette, 133
pimento, 84
provolone, Simple and Easy Porcini
 Mushroom Veggie Burgers, 94
ricotta
 Ratatouille Napoleon, 159–160
 Roasted Garlic and Ricotta Spread, 80
 Zucchini and Tomato Galette, 133
smoked Gouda, Butternut Squash Rotini Mac
 and Cheese, 175
Southern-Style Cheese Dip, 54
Vegetarian Roasted Red Pepper and Olive
 Muffuletta, 92
chef's knife, xv
cherry peppers, Natchitoches Umami Pies with
 Yogurt Chimichurri, 31
"chicken"
 Chicken-Fried Portobello with Mushroom
  and Shallot Gravy, 138–139
 "chicken" pot pie, 134
 Vegetarian "Chicken" and Waffles, 122
 Vegetarian "Chicken" with Parsley and Olive
  Oil Dumplings, 146
chickpea sandwich with blue cheese and
 tomato, 86
Chipotle BBQ Sauce, 226, 227
 BBQ Tofu Nachos with Chipotle Pinto Beans
  and Guacamole, 37
 BBQ Tofu Pizza, 140
 Lime Truck's Corn Cake with BBQ Slaw, 28–29
chipotle pepper
 Chipotle BBQ Sauce, 226
 Mexican Corn Chowder, 108

Chipotle Pinto Beans, BBQ Tofu Nachos with
 Chipotle Pinto Beans and Guacamole, 37, 38
chocolate
 chocolate hazelnut butter, xviii
 No-Bake Chipotle Chocolate Tart, 180
Chubby Vegetarian Gumbo, 111–112
Chubby Vegetarian Quick-Smoking
 Method, 231
cilantro, 108
 Vegetarian Country Captain, 119
coconut
 Smoked Coconut Bacon, 82
 Toasted Coconut Muffins, 22
coconut milk
 Curried Cauliflower Soup, 102
 Dirty Fried Rice, King Oyster Mushroom
  "Scallops," and Creole Coconut Sauce, 147
 Vegetarian Country Captain, 119
Collard Greens with Honey, Shallots, and
 Mushrooms, 72
condiments, xix
cookies
 cheddar-pecan, 33
 Rosemary-Lemon Cookies, 182
cooking wine, xxi
corn
 Charred Corn and Avocado Salsa, 233
 creamed, 28
 succotash, 143–144
 Vegetarian Frogmore Stew, 114
Corn Cake with BBQ Slaw, 28–29
corn chowder, Mexican, 108
corn grits, xvii
 Artichoke Hearts and Succotash over Smoked
  Cheddar Grits, 143
corn husks, 20-Minute Tamales, 126–127
corn tortilla chips, BBQ Tofu Nachos with
 Chipotle Pinto Beans and Guacamole, 37
cornbread
 Cheddar Jalapeño, use in salad, 62
 Smoked Cheddar Jalapeño Cornbread, 153
cornmeal, xvii
Cotija cheese, Mexican Corn Chowder, 108
cream, xix
 Strawberry-Basil Shortcake Sliders, 197
creamed corn, 28
crème fraîche, Mini Potato and Buttermilk
 Pancakes with Beluga Lentils and Crème
 Fraîche, 46

Creole mustard
    sauce, 41
        Southern Caesar Salad with Cornbread
            Croutons, 62
Crispy Eggplant Sandwiches and Roasted Garlic
   and Ricotta Spread, 79–80
crust. *See also* Basic Piecrust Dough
        Graham Cracker Crust, 180
cucumbers
        Juicer Bloody Marys, 214
        Spicy Cucumber-Lemonade Popsicles, 191
        Summer Salad, 65
Curried Cauliflower Soup, 102
curry, 119

dates, Smoked Dates Stuffed with Goat Cheese
   and Pecans, 53
desserts
        Bourbon Pecan Tart, 188
        Brown Rice and Brown Butter Crispies, 183
        Egg Custard Brûlée, 202
        Grilled Peach Ice Cream, 178
        Mascarpone Banana Pudding, 192
        Nannie's Blueberry Pie, 185
        Nannie's Pound Cake, 186
        No-Bake Chipotle Chocolate Tart, 180
        Olive Oil Shortbread with Salted Dark
          Chocolate Ganache, 195
        Rosemary-Lemon Cookies, 182
        Spicy Cucumber-Lemonade Popsicles, 191
        Strawberry-Basil Shortcake Sliders, 197–198
        Triple-Ginger Apple Crisp, 200–201
Deviled Egg and Olive, 58
Dirty Fried Rice, King Oyster Mushroom
   "Scallops," and Creole Coconut Sauce, 147–148
Donnelly, "Blackie," 54
dressing. *See also* sauce
        Honey-Tarragon Dressing, 67
drinks
        Bourbon with Basil and Lemonade Granita, 219
        Easy Horchata, 212
        Juicer Bloody Marys, 214
        Melonade, 217
        Peanut Butter and Banana Smoothie, 206
        Sazerac Iced Tea, 210
        Spinach and Strawberry Green Smoothie, 208
dry rub, Memphis BBQ Dry Rub, 225
dumplings, Vegetarian "Chicken" with Parsley and

        Olive Oil Dumplings, 146
Easy Horchata, 212
Easy Whipped Cream, 188
Egg Custard Brûlée, 202
egg drop soup, Saffron Egg Drop Soup, 105
eggplant
        Mushroom Meat, 230
        Ratatouille Napoleon, 159–160
        sandwiches, 79
        Vegetarian Country Captain, 119
        Vegetarian Red Beans and Rice with Andouille
          Eggplant, 170–171
eggs
        Chanterelle and Apricot Stuffed Acorn
          Squash with Miracle Mushroom Gravy, 136
        Deviled Egg and Olive, 58
        Dirty Fried Rice, 148
        Egg Custard Brûlée, 202
        egg wash, 31, 134
        Smoked Sun-Dried Tomato Tortilla with
          Herbed Aioli, 10
        Southern Benedict with Wilted Spinach and
          Espresso Redeye Gravy, 5–6
        Sweet Potato Grits with Maple Mushrooms
          and a Fried Egg, 3–4
        Vegetarian "Chicken" and Waffles, 122
        Vegetarian Meatballs, 154
        Vegetarian "Midnight Snack" Inspired by
          Restaurant Iris, 77

English, Kelly, 31, 77, 78
Expresso Redeye Gravy, 6

fats, xvii
filling, for tamales, 127
flours, xvii–xviii
food processor, xv, 167
French Toast Pancake, 18
Fried Chickpea Sandwich with Blue Cheese and
   Tomato, 86
Fried Green Tomato Po' Boy, 88–89
fritters
        chickpea, 86
        Okra Fritters with Creole Mustard Sauce, 41
Frogmore stew, 114
fruit, xxi
        apples
          Triple-Ginger Apple Crisp, 200

Vegetarian Country Captain, 119
apricots, Chanterelle and Apricot Stuffed
    Acorn Squash with Miracle Mushroom
    Gravy, 136
bananas
    Mascarpone Banana Pudding, 192
    Peanut Butter and Banana Smoothie, 206
    Spinach and Strawberry Green
      Smoothie, 208
    Super-Moist Banana Muffins, 20
blueberries, Nannie's Blueberry Pie, 185
cantaloupe, Melonade, 217
peaches
    Grilled Peach Ice Cream, 178
    Peach and Tarragon Pesto Pizza, 131
    Sweet Potato Pancakes with Peaches and
      Pecans, 17
watermelon
    Grilled Watermelon and Tomato Salad
      with Honey-Lime Vinaigrette, 61
    Melonade, 217
    Watermelon and Tomato Gazpacho, 106
frying pan, xv

galette
    Apple, Cheddar, and Thyme Galette, 14
    Zucchini and Tomato Galette, 133
ganache, Salted Dark Chocolate Ganache, 195
garbanzo beans
    garbanzo bean flour, xviii
    Vegetarian Country Captain, 119
garlic, xxi
    Chipotle BBQ Sauce, 226
    garlic mashed potatoes, 167
    Roasted Garlic and Ricotta Spread, 80
    Vegetable-Packed Tomato Sauce, 229
gazpacho, Watermelon and Tomato Gazpacho,
  106
ginger, Vegetarian Country Captain, 119
glaze, lemon, 186
goat cheese
    Butternut Squash Rotini Mac and Cheese, 175
    Fried Green Tomato Po' Boy, 88
    Grilled Watermelon and Tomato Salad with
      Honey-Lime Vinaigrette, 61
    Lemon Zest and Thyme Pimento Cheese, 84
    mushroom stuffing, 128–129
    Peach and Tarragon Pesto Pizza, 131

Roast Beet Salad with Sea Salt Granola and
    Honey-Tarragon Dressing, 67
Simple Smoke Migas Bowl, 12
Smoked Dates Stuffed with Goat Cheese and
    Pecans, 53
Graham Cracker Crust, 180
granola, Sea Salt Granola, 232
grater, xvi
gravy
    Expresso Redeye Gravy, 6
    Miracle Mushroom Gravy, 8
    Mushroom and Shallot Gravy, 138–139
Greek yogurt
    Honeyed Yogurt, 201
    Peanut Butter and Banana Smoothie, 206
    Yogurt Chimichurri, 32
Green Pea Hummus, 39
green peppers
    Chubby Vegetarian Gumbo, 111
    Vegetarian Country Captain, 119
greens, Collard Greens with Honey, Shallots, and
  Mushrooms, 72
Grilled Peach Ice Cream, 178
Grilled Watermelon and Tomato Salad with
  Honey-Lime Vinaigrette, 61
grits
    Artichoke Hearts and Succotash over Smoked
      Cheddar Grits, 143
    Sweet Potato Grits with Maple Mushrooms
      and a Fried Egg, 3–4

Hawkins, Chris, 37
Herbed Aioli, 10
honey, xix
    Collard Greens with Honey, Shallots, and
      Mushrooms, 72
    honey-lime vinaigrette, 61
    Honey-Tarragon Dressing, 67
honeydew melon, Melonade, 217
Honeyed Yogurt, 201
Hoppin' John Black-Eyed Pea Butter, 56
horchata, easy, 212
Hughes, Michael, 43
hummus, Green Pea Hummus, 39

ice cream, Grilled Peach Ice Cream, 178
ice-cream scoops, xvi
iced tea, Sazerac Iced Tea, 210

jalapeño
    Juicer Bloody Marys, 214
    Simple Smoky Salsa, 223
    Smoked Cheddar Jalapeño Cornbread, 153
    Vegetarian Country Captain, 119
    Watermelon and Tomato Gazpacho, 106
jam, strawberry, 197, 198
jars
    caprese salad in, 70
    Mascarpone Banana Pudding in, 192
jasmine rice, xviii
    Chubby Vegetarian Gumbo, 111
    Vegetarian Country Captain, 119
jelly, Sambal Pepper Jelly, 33
Juicer Bloody Marys, 214

ketchup
    Chipotle BBQ Sauce, 226
    ketchup glaze, 167
Kimball, Jesse, 82
kitchen tools, xv–xvi
kombu (dried seaweed), 46, 47

leeks, mushroom stuffing, 128–129
lemon zest
    lemon glaze, 186
    Lemon Zest and Thyme Pimento Cheese, 84
    Rosemary-Lemon Cookies, 182
lemons, xxi
    Bourbon with Basil and Lemonade Granita, 219
    Melonade, 217
    Spicy Cucumber-Lemonade Popsicles, 191
lentils, xviii
    Porcini and Portobello Mushroom
        Bourguignon over Smashed Potatoes,
        163–164
    Tacos with Spicy, Smoky Lentils, 125
lettuce
    BBQ Tofu Nachos with Chipotle Pinto Beans
        and Guacamole, 37
    romaine
        Southern Caesar Salad with Cornbread
            Croutons, 62
        Vegetarian Roasted Red Pepper and Olive
            Muffuletta, 92
lime
    honey-lime vinaigrette, 61
    Melonade, 217

Lime Truck's Corn Cake with BBQ Slaw, 28–29
liquid measuring cup, xv
liquid smoke, xix

main courses
    20-Minute Tamales, 126–127
    Artichoke Hearts and Succotash over Smoked
        Cheddar Grits, 143–144
    BBQ Tofu Pizza, 140
    Butternut Squash Rotini Mac and Cheese, 175
    Chanterelle and Apricot Stuffed Acorn
        Squash with Miracle Mushroom Gravy, 136
    Chicken-Fried Portobello with Mushroom and
        Shallot Gravy, 138–139
    Dirty Fried Rice, King Oyster Mushroom
        "Scallops," and Creole Coconut Sauce,
        147–148
    Memphis-Style Dry Rub BBQ Tofu, 173
    Peach and Tarragon Pesto Pizza, 131
    Porcini and Portobello Mushroom
        Bourguignon over Smashed Potatoes,
        163–164
    Ratatouille Napoleon, 159–160
    Smoked Cheddar Jalapeño Cornbread, 153
    Stuffed Portobello Mushroom Wellington,
        128–129
    Tacos with Spicy, Smoky Lentils, 125
    Tofu Almondine in a White Wine-Butter
        Sauce, 157–158
    Vegan Peanut Chili with Charred Corn and
        Avocado Salsa, 162
    Vegetarian Boudin Sausage, 151
    Vegetarian "Chicken" and Waffles, 122–123
    Vegetarian "Chicken" Pot Pie, 134
    Vegetarian "Chicken" with Parsley and Olive
        Oil Dumplings, 146
    Vegetarian Country Captain, 119–120
    Vegetarian Meatballs, 154
    Vegetarian Meatloaf with Garlic Mashed
        Potatoes, 166–168
    Vegetarian Red Beans and Rice with Andouille
        Eggplant, 170–171
    Zucchini and Tomato Galette, 133
Maldon sea salt flakes, xx
manchego cheese
    Peach and Tarragon Pesto Pizza, 131
    Saffron Egg Drop Soup, 105
marshmallows, vegan, 183

masa, 20-Minute Tamales, 126–127
Mascarpone Banana Pudding, 192
mascarpone cheese, Mascarpone Banana
    Pudding, 192
measuring cups, xv
measuring spoons, xv
meatballs, vegetarian, 154
meatloaf, Vegetarian Meatloaf with Garlic Mashed
    Potatoes, 166–168
Melonade, 217
Memphis BBQ Dry Rub, 225
        for BBQ Portobello Mushroom Sandwich with
            Smoked Gouda, 91
Memphis-Style Dry Rub BBQ Tofu, 173
meringue, 192
Mexican Corn Chowder, 108
milk, xix
Mini Potato and Buttermilk Pancakes with Beluga
    Lentils and Crème Fraîche, 46–47
Miracle Mushroom Gravy, 8
        for Chanterelle and Apricot Stuffed Acorn
            Squash, 136
mozzarella, BBQ Tofu Pizza, 140
muffins
        Super-Moist Banana Muffins, 20
        Toasted Coconut Muffins, 22
        Vegan Bran Muffins, 24
muffuletta
        Vegetarian Roasted Red Pepper and Olive
            Muffuletta, 92
mushrooms
        button
            Collard Greens with Honey, Shallots, and
                Mushrooms, 72
            Dirty Fried Rice, 148
        chanterelle, Chanterelle and Apricot Stuffed
            Acorn Squash, 136
        crimini
            Chubby Vegetarian Gumbo, 111
            Ratatouille Napoleon, 159–160
            Sweet Potato Grits with Maple
                Mushrooms and a Fried Egg, 3–4
            Vegetarian Meatloaf with Garlic Mashed
                Potatoes, 166–168
        king oyster, Dirty Fried Rice, King Oyster
            Mushroom "Scallops," and Creole Coconut
            Sauce, 147
        Mushroom Meat, 230
            for meatballs, 154

        for tamale filling, 127
    Oyster Mushroom Rockefeller, 43
    porcini mushroom broth, 164
    portobello
        BBQ Portobello Mushroom Sandwich with
            Smoked Gouda, 91
        Chicken-Fried Portobello with Mushroom
            and Shallot Gravy, 138–139
        Expresso Redeye Gravy, 6
        Porcini and Portobello Mushroom
            Bourguignon over Smashed Potatoes,
            163–164
        Simple and Easy Porcini Mushroom Veggie
            Burgers, 94
        Smoky Grilled Vegetable Quesadillas, 99
        Stuffed Portobello Mushroom Wellington,
            128–129
    Vegan Sloppy Joes, 97
    in vegetarian broth, 228
    Vegetarian "Midnight Snack" Inspired by
        Restaurant Iris, 77
mustard, Creole mustard sauce, 41
mustard pan sauce, spicy, 144

Nannie's Blueberry Pie, 185
Nannie's Pound Cake, 186
Natchitoches Umami Pies with Yogurt
    Chimichurri, 31–32
N'awlins sauce, 89
Neufchâtel cheese, Nannie's Pound Cake, 186
No-Bake Chipotle Chocolate Tart, 180
No-Bones-About-It Vegetarian Broth, 228
No-Fuss Guacamole, BBQ Tofu Nachos with
    Chipotle Pinto Beans and Guacamole, 37–38
nuts, xviii
    almonds, xviii
        Sea Salt Granola, 232
        Tofu Almondine in a White Wine-Butter
            Sauce, 157–158
        Vegetarian Country Captain, 119
    peanuts, Vegan Peanut Chili with Charred
        Corn and Avocado Salsa, 162
    pecans, xviii
        Bourbon Pecan Tart, 188
        Cheddar-Pecan Cookies, 33–34
        Sea Salt Granola, 232
        Smoked Dates Stuffed with Goat Cheese
            and Pecans, 53

Sweet Potato Pancakes with Peaches
and Pecans, 17
Warm Brussels Sprout Salad with Smoked
Feta and Candied Pecans, 68
walnuts, xviii
tarragon pesto, 131

oats
Oat Streusel Topping, 200
Sea Salt Granola, 232
Oaxaca cheese
Smoky Grilled Vegetable Quesadillas, 99
Southern-Style Cheese Dip, 54
okra
Chubby Vegetarian Gumbo, 111
Juicer Bloody Marys, 214
Okra Fritters with Creole Mustard Sauce, 41
succotash, 143–144
olive oil, xvii
Olive Oil Shortbread with Salted Dark
Chocolate Ganache, 195
olives
Deviled Egg and Olive, 58
olive tapenade, 160
Vegetarian Roasted Red Pepper and Olive
Muffuletta, 92
onions, xxi
Chanterelle and Apricot Stuffed Acorn
Squash with Miracle Mushroom Gravy, 136
Charred Corn and Avocado Salsa, 233
Chipotle BBQ Sauce, 226
Chubby Vegetarian Gumbo, 111
Curried Cauliflower Soup, 102
Mexican Corn Chowder, 108
Mushroom Meat, 230
porcini mushroom broth, 164
Ratatouille Napoleon, 159–160
Tacos with Spicy, Smoky Lentils, 125
Vegan Peanut Chili with Charred Corn and
Avocado Salsa, 162
Vegetable-Packed Tomato Sauce, 229
Vegetarian Boudin Sausage, 151
Vegetarian Red Beans and Rice with Andouille
Eggplant, 170
orange juice, Spinach and Strawberry Green
Smoothie, 208
oranges, Sazerac Iced Tea, 210
outdoor grill, xvi

Oyster Mushroom Rockefeller, 43–44

pancake mix, Lime Truck's Corn Cake with BBQ
Slaw, 28–29
pancakes
French Toast Pancake, 18
Mini Potato and Buttermilk Pancakes with
Beluga Lentils and Crème Fraîche, 46
Sweet Potato Pancakes with Peaches and
Pecans, 17
parchment paper, xvi
parmesan cheese
Crispy Eggplant Sandwiches and Roasted
Garlic and Ricotta Spread, 79
Oyster Mushroom Rockefeller, 43
Roasted Garlic and Ricotta Spread, 80
Southern Caesar Salad with Cornbread
Croutons, 62
Vegetarian Meatballs, 154
Zucchini and Tomato Galette, 133
parsley, xxi
Green Pea Hummus, 39
Herbed Aioli, 10
parsley and tomato salad, 168
parsley and tomato topping, 4
Yogurt Chimichurri, 32
pasta, xviii
peaches
Grilled Peach Ice Cream, 178
Peach and Tarragon Pesto Pizza, 131
Sweet Potato Pancakes with Peaches and
Pecans, 17
peanut butter, xviii
Peanut Butter and Banana Smoothie, 206
peanuts, Vegan Peanut Chili with Charred Corn
and Avocado Salsa, 162
peas
succotash, 143–144
Vegetarian "Chicken" Pot Pie, 134
pecans, xviii
Bourbon Pecan Tart, 188
Cheddar-Pecan Cookies, 33–34
Sea Salt Granola, 232
Smoked Dates Stuffed with Goat Cheese and
Pecans, 53
Sweet Potato Pancakes with Peaches and
Pecans, 17
Warm Brussels Sprout Salad with Smoked

Feta and Candied Pecans, 68
peeler, xvi
pepper, xx–xxi
peppers. *See* green peppers; poblano peppers; red pepper
phyllo dough
    Ratatouille Napoleon, 159–160
    Stuffed Portobello Mushroom Wellington, 128–129
pies
    Basic Piecrust Dough, 227
        Bourbon Pecan Tart, 188
        Nannie's Blueberry Pie, 185
        Vegetarian "Chicken" Pot Pie, 134
        Zucchini and Tomato Galette, 133
    Nannie's Blueberry Pie, 185
pimento cheese, 84
pinto beans
    Chipotle Pinto Beans, 38
    Vegan Peanut Chili with Charred Corn and Avocado Salsa, 162
pizza
    BBQ Tofu Pizza, 140
    Beer Pizza Crust, 224
pizza stone, xvi
poblano peppers
    Smoky Grilled Vegetable Quesadillas, 99
    Southern-Style Cheese Dip, 54
popsicles, Spicy Cucumber-Lemonade Popsicles, 191
Porcini and Portobello Mushroom Bourguignon over Smashed Potatoes, 163–164
potatoes, xxi
    garlic mashed potatoes, 167
    Porcini and Portobello Mushroom Bourguignon over Smashed Potatoes, 163–164
    potato pancakes, 46
    Smoked Sun-Dried Tomato Tortilla with Herbed Aioli, 10
    Vegetarian "Chicken" Pot Pie, 134
    Vegetarian Country Captain, 119
    Vegetarian Frogmore Stew, 114
pound cake, Nannie's Pound Cake, 186
produce, xxi
protein, nuts for, xviii
provolone cheese, Simple and Easy Porcini Mushroom Veggie Burgers, 94
pudding, Mascarpone Banana Pudding, 192

pumpkin seeds, Sea Salt Granola, 232

quesadillas, Smoky Grilled Vegetable Quesadillas, 99
Quick Smoking Method
    for coconut flakes, 82
    sun-dried tomatoes from, 10
Quinn, Jason, 28

rapid-rise yeast, xx
Ratatouille Napoleon, 159–160
red beans
    Chubby Vegetarian Gumbo, 111
    Vegetarian Red Beans and Rice with Andouille Eggplant, 170
red pepper
    Chubby Vegetarian Gumbo, 111
    Vegetarian Roasted Red Pepper and Olive Muffuletta, 92
rémoulade sauce, 77, 78
rice, xviii
    Brown Rice and Brown Butter Crispies, 183
    Dirty Fried Rice, 148
    Vegan Peanut Chili with Charred Corn and Avocado Salsa, 162
    Vegetarian Boudin Sausage, 151
rice milk, Easy Horchata, 212
ricotta cheese
    Ratatouille Napoleon, 159–160
    Roasted Garlic and Ricotta Spread, 80
    Zucchini and Tomato Galette, 133
Roast Beet Salad with Sea Salt Granola and Honey-Tarragon Dressing, 67
Roasted Garlic and Ricotta Spread, 80
romaine lettuce
    Southern Caesar Salad with Cornbread Croutons, 62
    Vegetarian Roasted Red Pepper and Olive Muffuletta, 92
Rosemary-Lemon Cookies, 182

Saffron Egg Drop Soup, 105
salads
    Caprese Salad in a Jar, 70
    Collard Greens with Honey, Shallots, and Mushrooms, 72
    Grilled Watermelon and Tomato Salad with Honey-Lime Vinaigrette, 61

parsley and tomato salad, 168

Roast Beet Salad with Sea Salt Granola and Honey-Tarragon Dressing, 67

Southern Caesar Salad with Cornbread Croutons, 62

Summer Salad, 65

Warm Brussels Sprout Salad with Smoked Feta and Candied Pecans, 68

salsa

Charred Corn and Avocado Salsa, 233

Simple Smoky Salsa, 223

salt, xx–xxi

salted butter, xvii

Salted Dark Chocolate Ganache, 195

Sambal Pepper Jelly and Savory Cheddar-Pecan Cookies, 33–34

sandwiches

BBQ Portobello Mushroom Sandwich with Smoked Gouda, 91

Crispy Eggplant Sandwiches and Roasted Garlic and Ricotta Spread, 79–80

Fried Chickpea Sandwich with Blue Cheese and Tomato, 86

Fried Green Tomato Po' Boy, 88–89

Lemon Zest and Thyme Pimento Cheese, 84

Simple and Easy Porcini Mushroom Veggie Burgers, 94

Smoked Coconut Bacon, 82

Smoky Grilled Vegetable Quesadillas, 99

Vegan Sloppy Joes, 97

Vegetarian "Midnight Snack" Inspired by Restaurant Iris, 77–78

Vegetarian Roasted Red Pepper and Olive Muffuletta, 92

sauce, xix

Chipotle BBQ Sauce, 226

N'awlins, 89

Spicy Mustard Pan Sauce, 144

Vegetable-Packed Tomato Sauce, 229

white wine-butter sauce, 158

saucepan, xvi

sausage

vegetarian boudin, 151

Vegetarian Frogmore Stew, 114

Sazerac Iced Tea, 210

Sea Salt Granola, 232

Roast Beet Salad with, 67

Seasoned Black Beans, 12

seitan

Vegetarian "Chicken" Pot Pie, 134

Vegetarian "Chicken" with Parsley and Olive Oil Dumplings, 146

shallots, xxi

Collard Greens with Honey, Shallots, and Mushrooms, 72

Dirty Fried Rice, 148

Mushroom and Shallot Gravy, 138–139

olive tapenade, 160

Oyster Mushroom Rockefeller, 43

parsley and tomato salad, 168

Simple and Easy Porcini Mushroom Veggie Burgers, 94

succotash, 143–144

Vegetarian "Chicken" Pot Pie, 134

shortbread, Olive Oil Shortbread with Salted Dark Chocolate Ganache, 195

shrimp, artichoke hearts as substitute, 143

Simple and Easy Porcini Mushroom Veggie Burgers, 94

Simple Smoky Migas Bowl, 12

Simple Smoky Salsa, 223

in Simple Smoky Migas Bowl, 12

Simply Smoky Salsa, for 20-Minute Tamales, 126–127

sloppy joes, vegan, 97

Smoked Cheddar Jalapeño Cornbread, 153

Smoked Coconut Bacon, 82

Smoked Dates Stuffed with Goat Cheese and Pecans, 53

smoked feta, Warm Brussels Sprout Salad with Smoked Feta and Candied Pecans, 68

smoked gouda

BBQ Portobello Mushroom Sandwich with Smoked Gouda, 91

Butternut Squash Rotini Mac and Cheese, 175

Smoked Sun-Dried Tomato Tortilla with Herbed Aioli, 10

smoking, xix

Chubby Vegetarian Quick-Smoking Method, 231

Smoky Grilled Vegetable Quesadillas, 99

smoothies

Peanut Butter and Banana Smoothie, 206

Spinach and Strawberry Green Smoothie, 208

soups

Chubby Vegetarian Gumbo, 111–112

Curried Cauliflower Soup, 102

Mexican Corn Chowder, 108

Saffron Egg Drop Soup, 105
Triple Tomato Soup with Toasted White
    Cheddar Crouton, 100
Vegetarian Frogmore Stew, 114–115
Watermelon and Tomato Gazpacho, 106
Southern Benedict with Wilted Spinach and
    Espresso Redeye Gravy, 5–6
Southern Caesar Salad with Cornbread
    Croutons, 62
Southern-Style Cheese Dip, 54
soy milk, Peanut Butter and Banana Smoothie, 206
Spectrum Olive Oil Mayonnaise, xix
spices, xx
Spicy Cucumber-Lemonade Popsicles, 191
Spicy Mustard Pan Sauce, 144
spinach
    Fried Chickpea Sandwich with Blue Cheese
        and Tomato, 86
    Oyster Mushroom Rockefeller, 43
    Spinach and Strawberry Green Smoothie, 208
    wilted, 5
starches, xvii–xviii
stock, xxi
stockpot, xv
strawberries
    Spinach and Strawberry Green Smoothie, 208
    Strawberry-Basil Shortcake Sliders, 197–198
    Strawberry Jam, 197, 198
streusel topping, oat, 200
stuffed peppers, Lemon Zest and Thyme Pimento
    Cheese for, 84
Stuffed Portobello Mushroom Wellington, 128–129
stuffing, for mushrooms, 128–129
succotash, Artichoke Hearts and Succotash over
    Smoked Cheddar Grits, 143
sugar, xix
Summer Salad, 65
Super-Moist Banana Muffins, 20
sweet potatoes, xxi
    Natchitoches Umami Pies with Yogurt
        Chimichurri, 31
    Sweet Potato Grits with Maple Mushrooms
        and a Fried Egg, 3–4
    Sweet Potato Pancakes with Peaches and
        Pecans, 17
sweetener, xix

Tacos with Spicy, Smoky Lentils, 125

tamales, 20-Minute Tamales, 126–127
tarragon pesto, Peach and Tarragon Pesto Pizza, 131
tea, Sazerac Iced Tea, 210
Tellicherry black peppercorns, xx–xxi
tempeh
    Simple and Easy Porcini Mushroom Veggie
        Burgers, 94
    Vegetarian Meatloaf with Garlic Mashed
        Potatoes, 166–168
thyme, xxi
    Apple, Cheddar, and Thyme Galette, 14
Toasted Coconut Muffins, 22
tofu
    BBQ Tofu Nachos with Chipotle Pinto Beans
        and Guacamole, 37
    Memphis-Style Dry Rub BBQ Tofu, 173
    No-Bake Chipotle Chocolate Tart, 180
    Tofu Almondine in a White Wine-Butter
        Sauce, 157–158
    Tofu and Truffle "Pork" Rinds, 49
tomato paste, xix
tomato tortilla, Smoked Sun-Dried Tomato Tortilla
    with Herbed Aioli, 10
tomatoes
    Chipotle Pinto Beans, 38
    Chubby Vegetarian Gumbo, 111
    Fried Chickpea Sandwich with Blue Cheese
        and Tomato, 86
    Fried Green Tomato Po' Boy, 88
    Grilled Watermelon and Tomato Salad with
        Honey-Lime Vinaigrette, 61
    Juicer Bloody Marys, 214
    parsley and tomato salad, 168
    Saffron Egg Drop Soup, 105
    Simple Smoky Salsa, 223
    Southern-Style Cheese Dip, 54
    Summer Salad, 65
    sun-dried
        Dirty Fried Rice, 148
        Smoked Sun-Dried Tomato Tortilla with
            Herbed Aioli, 10
        Tacos with Spicy, Smoky Lentils, 125
        Triple Tomato Soup with Toasted White
            Cheddar Crouton, 100
        Vegetarian Boudin Sausage, 151
        Vegetarian Meatloaf with Garlic Mashed
            Potatoes, 166–168
        Vegetarian Red Beans and Rice with
            Andouille Eggplant, 170

Vegan Peanut Chili with Charred Corn and
  Avocado Salsa, 162
Vegetable-Packed Tomato Sauce, 50, 229
Vegetarian Country Captain, 119
Vegetarian Roasted Red Pepper and Olive
  Muffuletta, 92
Watermelon and Tomato Gazpacho, 106
Zucchini and Tomato Galette, 133
tongs, xvi
toppings
  parsley and tomato, 4
  for Toasted Coconut Muffins, 22
  for Vegan Bran Muffins, 24
tortillas, Smoked Sun-Dried Tomato Tortilla with
  Herbed Aioli, 10
Triple-Ginger Apple Crisp, 200–201
Triple Tomato Soup with Toasted White Cheddar
  Crouton, 100

unsalted butter, xvii

vanilla beans, xx
vanilla wafers, Mascarpone Banana Pudding, 192
Vegan Bran Muffins, 24
Vegan Peanut Chili with Charred Corn and
  Avocado Salsa, 162
Vegan Sloppy Joes, 97
vegetable broth, No-Bones-About-It Vegetarian
  Broth, 228
Vegetable-Packed Tomato Sauce, 229
  for BBQ Tofu Pizza, 140
  for Crispy Eggplant Sandwiches and Roasted
    Garlic and Ricotta Spread, 79
  for Vegetarian Meatballs, 154
  for Zucchini Fries, 50
vegetable shortening, xvii
vegetable smoking device, 53
Vegetarian Boudin Sausage, 151
Vegetarian "Chicken" and Waffles, 122–123
Vegetarian "Chicken" Pot Pie, 134
Vegetarian "Chicken" with Parsley and Olive Oil
  Dumplings, 146
Vegetarian Country Captain, 119–120
Vegetarian Frogmore Stew, 114–115
vegetarian gumbo, 111
Vegetarian Meatballs, 154
Vegetarian Meatloaf with Garlic Mashed Potatoes,
  166–168

Vegetarian "Midnight Snack" Inspired by
  Restaurant Iris, 77–78
Vegetarian Red Beans and Rice with Andouille
  Eggplant, 170–171
Vegetarian Roasted Red Pepper and Olive
  Muffuletta, 92
vinaigrette
  balsamic, 70
  honey-lime, 61
vinegar, xx
vodka, Juicer Bloody Marys, 214

waffles, Vegetarian "Chicken" and Waffles, 122–123
walnuts, xviii
  tarragon pesto, 131
Warm Brussels Sprout Salad with Smoked Feta
  and Candied Pecans, 68
watermelon
  Grilled Watermelon and Tomato Salad with
    Honey-Lime Vinaigrette, 61
  Melonade, 217
  Watermelon and Tomato Gazpacho, 106
wheat gluten, Vegetarian Boudin Sausage, 151
whipping cream, Easy Whipped Cream, 188
white wine
  Vegan Peanut Chili with Charred Corn and
    Avocado Salsa, 162
  Vegetable-Packed Tomato Sauce, 229
  white wine-butter sauce, 158
wilted spinach, 5
wine, cooking, xxi
Worcestershire sauce, xix

yeast, rapid-rise, xx
yogurt
  honeyed, 201
  Yogurt Chimichurri, 32
Yukon Gold potatoes, xxi

Zatarain's Creole Mustard, xix
zester, xvi
zucchini
  Chubby Vegetarian Gumbo, 111
  tarragon pesto, 131
  Zucchini and Tomato Galette, 133
  Zucchini Fries, 50